BEKKS

THE

BIZARRE

CHARLES J. ADAMS III

EXETER HOUSE BOOKS
Reading, Pennsylvania
1995

BERKS THE BIZARRE
©1995 Charles J. Adams III
Published by EXETER HOUSE BOOKS

Stories in this volume appeared originally in the *READING
EAGLE*. Used with permission.

FIRST EDITION
PRINTED IN THE UNITED STATES OF AMERICA

ISBN 1-880683-06-7

TABLE OF CONTENTS

ACKNOWLEDGEMENTS

The author is grateful to the *Reading Eagle* newspaper, in which the majority of these stories were originally published under the column head of "Berks the Bizarre."
Particular thanks are due to Larry Miller, the patient editor of the Sunday edition, who kept the author quite aware of deadlines; to Charles M. "Chuck" Gallagher, the *Eagle's* managing editor, who sanctioned this compilation; *Reading Eagle* and *Reading Times* illustrator George M. Arentz, whose very effective artwork accompanied the newspaper columns and these pages; and to beloved daughter Emily J. Adams, who suffered through the proofreading process and assured me that no misteak got by hur.
A special note of thanks to the readers of the newspaper feature and this book, and to those who shared their personal experiences with the author, and thus, all who chose to explore Berks...the Bizarre!

BERKS THE BIZARRE
THE MAN, THE MYSTERY, THE LONG LOST FRIEND

The man was as much a mystery and enigma as his legacy.

Precious little is known about his life. What he left for all eternity to ponder is cloaked in a shadowy realm somehwere between what is natural and what is *super*natural.

He could be considered what his legacy was entitled: *Der Lan Verbogene Freund.*

He was Johann Georg Hohmann, and to practitioners of what some call "white witchcraft," he was a master craftsman and chronicler.

It has been fairly well documented that Hohmann was born in Germany in 1775.

At age 27, he emigrated to the United States, landing in Philadelphia with his wife, Catherine, and son, Caspar. They came in indentured servitude and were purchased by a Bucks County family.

To pay off his debts, Hohmann wandered throughout southeastern Pennsylvania, trading his calligraphic and artistic talents for sustenance and cash.

He illustrated, illuminated and lettered family documents, and was said to have been skilled at the intricate art form known as *fraktur*. His main source of income was from *taufscheins*, a form of illuminated baptismal certificates.

A devout Catholic, Hohmann collected prayers, potions and superstitions along his way.

By 1819, his own philosophy and theology

I

BERKS THE BIZARRE

became tightly intertwined with the eclectic sampling of cures, curses and verses he had gathered in his itinerancy.

Just how he came to actually publish his own book is unknown. But, in 1819, hoping for financial and spiritual gain, "Der Lang Verbonene Freund," (The Long Lost Friend) was printed and distributed.

Published in German, the book emerged from a press somewhere in Reading.

It is believed Hohmann may have had access to a printing press and may have done the job by himself. This factual gap in his story is but one of many.

A rambling mixture of thoughts and processes gleaned from such diverse sources as the Hebrew *cabala*, Egyptian hieroglyphics and the deep mysticism of the Germans, the Gypsies and the Druids, "The Long Lost Friend" circulated quietly in the underground of early nineteenth century society.

It offered strange cures, protections and precautions. Some believed it was a manual of hexes, curses and spells. Hohmann denied that belief.

Material included in the volume was included in a strange kind of faith healing known as "pow-wow." The origin of the name is obscure. Some say it was named after the classic name for a Native American gathering, while others claim it is a corruption of the word "power."

What is remarkable about Hohmann's thin volume is that it has not been out of print since the day it was first released. The first edition in English was published around 1855.

In 1928, the book gained certain notoriety when it figured in the "Hex Murder" of York County.

BERKS THE BIZARRE

A man who felt he had been cursed by another determined that the only way to break the curse was to steal the other's copy of "The Long Lost Friend."

The aggrieved man wound up killing the alleged "witch" instead.

Hohmann never realized any real monetary gain from his effort. Six years after the book was published, his modest farm went under the sheriff's gavel.

While pow-wow is still practiced by a very few, it has been relegated mostly to folklore. The medical community rebuts and scoffs at it. Religious leaders ignore or deny its powers.

Hohmann's book is considered either an historic novelty or a hornbook of healing, depending on the reader's outlook.

No matter, the curative offerings make for interesting reading.

Consider Hohmann's remedy for hair loss: "Pound up peach kernels, mix with vinegar and put on the bald place."

Or, for warts, try roasting chicken feet and rubbing the warts with them. Then, bury the roasted feet under the eaves of your home.

A simple precaution against injuries is to carry the right eye of a wolf inside your right sleeve.

Some cures had curious codicils.

In his "Remedy for Epilepsy, Provided the Subject Had Never Fallen Into Fire or Water," Hohmann suggested the victim write "IT IS ALL OVER" backwards on paper one time.

They then must put the paper in a scarlet cloth and wrap it in unbleached linen. *Then*, they must hang the bundle around their neck on the first Friday of the

BERKS THE BIZARRE

New Moon.

The books suggested ways to catch bigger fish, to cure worms (in both men and cattle), and to ease ailments ranging from toothaches to tapeworms.

Sometimes, there were options.

To stop bleeding, either recite, "Jesus Christ, dearest blood, that stoppeth the pain and stoppeth the blood," or count backward from 50. When the number three was reached, Hohmann said, the bleeding would stop.

Among the most baffling, and yet the simplest, of the remedies is one for the sniffles.

"Whenever you pull off your shoes and stockings, run your fingers in between all the toes and smell it. This will certainly effect a cure."

Uh, yeah!

There are those who have probed far deeper into Hohmann's life and legend who feel they have either tied up loose ends or untied tangled knots of misinformation.

These historians are to be lauded for their work, and that work should be added to the relatively scant information which has been recorded about the man's life and labors.

While little has been documented about Hohmann, he remains one of the most intriguing figures in the long, dark shadow cast by history.

BB

BERKS THE BIZARRE

THE NOCTURNAL MYSTERY

The night was clear and the moon was bright that warm, humid August night in 1875.

The silvery orb hovered over the Blue Mountains of Northern Berks County, casting the high ridges in dark shadows above Hamburg.

Folks across the county ventured outdoors shortly after nine o'clock that night as word spread: Something very unusual, very bizarre, was taking place in the sky!

Craning their necks skyward, people from Reading to Port Clinton and all points east and west watched in dazzled amazement.

The moon dominated the night skyscape as it always has. The constellation of Orion shone in pinpoint clarity nearby. Between these two celestial mainstays, however, loomed something most unexpected and untoward.

Skywatchers were startled, and hard-pressed to

5

explain the sight...and the sounds.

"There was a strange noise," said a Pottsville man who paused along the Centre Turnpike near Mohrsville to gawk. "A buzzing, humming sound seemed to come from the heavens, and I at the time imagined that it sounded like the hum of a steam fire engine."

Franklin Sherer, whose interpretation of the phenomenon may or may not have been tainted by a couple hours in a Reading tavern, emerged from that pub to witness what he later described as "a very bright place in the sky which kept moving and whirling so that I got dizzy."

Sherer offered an explanation, and reasoned the worst: "I think it was the reflection of the nebula of the moon against the penumbra of a planet, and it means an epidemic, or war, or something bad."

Others around the county imagined the mysterious display as the harbinger of evil or catastrophe. "It remained suspended near the known moon as another unknown satellite," testified a Hamburg woman. "I, too, heard a clear and distinct sound, as if to emanate from this body. There was no doubt to me that it was of another world, perhaps sinister or a portent of evil."

In a sense, it was an unenlightened age. Of course, heavenly phenomena were not new, but as the Industrial Revolution churned on, new and daring interpretations arose.

"This, this *thing*, seemed to glisten or glow in the night sky," another witness explained. "I could only imagine it was from, or indeed *was*, another world."

Still another man said, "It looked as if another, but

BERKS THE BIZARRE

smaller, earth was coming into view."

A mild panic may have overspread the rural expanses of Berks. With the unaided eye, the precise form and detail of the "thing" was barely perceptible.

A woman in Port Clinton was resourceful, and shed some rational light on the mystery.

"It was about nine o'clock that night," she reported, "when the heavens presented a most curious appearance. In getting out my magnifying glasses, I found that something very much like a rainbow appeared between the moon and the constellation of Orion. The colors of the rainbow were visible to the naked eye, but with the aid of glasses, you could discern thousands of smaller points of the supposed rainbow, new star, or planet.

"We watched the strange visitor until after eleven o'clock, when it began to gradually disappear."

As the sky, and observing heads, cleared, it became more obvious that the "strange visitor" was probably nothing more than a nocturnal rainbow--rare, but hardly threatening.

O.D. Schock, of Hamburg, felt he had identified the hitherto unidentified glowing object. "It was nothing extraordinary or calculated to create excitement or alarm, as rainbows in the night have been seen before."

Elaborating on this observation, another man theorized, "Rainbows have been observed at night. They arise from refractions and dispersion of the colored rays of the moon in the drops of rain; they are, however, very faint and usually form only white and yellow bows which were the colors I saw principally that night. The bow was not a large one, hence I can

7

easily imagine why many people imagined it to be another world, looming in the distance."

BB

A SAINTLY SPIRIT?

Residents of 229 South Fifth Street in Reading have reported the presence of a spirit in the building.

What's more, they say it could very well be a Saintly Spirit!

The tale is told that then-Bishop (now Saint) John Neumann stayed in the dwelling while on a visit to St. Peter's Convent and School. His presence was so overpowering, they claim, that a bit of him may remain.

Three separate tenants of the house have identified what could best be described as an "entity" at the base of the stairway.

"He doesn't do anything," one person said, "he just stands there." When asked to describe who the "he" is or was, the individual said, "I can't say for sure, of course, and although it sounds silly, I get the feeling it is somehow connected to Saint John Neumann."

A cat-sitter called in for work on one occasion begged off, saying she felt an eerie feeling in the place.

A recent owner was not convinced there was anything ghostly going on in the pleasant home, but did admit, "I must confess that when I first came into the house, I did feel something."

Whether that feeling has anything whatsoever to do with Saint John Neumann remains a mystery to those who have experienced it.

BB

BERKS THE BIZARRE
THE JERSEY DEVIL
VISITS BERKS COUNTY

It is one of the most enduring legends in the m[i]
Atlantic states. In its own way, it ranks right up th[e]
with the Loch Ness Monster of Scotland, the Yeti
the Himalayas, Bigfoot of America's northwest, a[
the Monster of Boggy Hollow in Arkansas.

It is the Jersey Devil.

And this is the story of the day the nefario[
creature borne of the New Jersey wilderness show[e]
its fearsome face in Reading.

The monstrous beast has been bounding in an[
out of regional folklore for two centuries.

Some say the Jersey Devil first surfaced along th[
lonely beaches of South Jersey, where it befriende[
the headless ghost of a pirate knave who was slain b[
Captain Kidd and left to guard his buried treasure.

The more accepted origin of the Devil is in
desolate reach of Atlantic County known as Leed[
Point.

In the wetlands between Smithville and Grea[
Bay, and on the edge of the modern-day Brigantin[
National Wildlife Refuge, Leeds Point is named after
Mrs. Leeds who, as the story goes, was barely scrapin[
by with a dozen children when she found out she was
to give birth to yet another.

She cursed this 13th birth, and cried so all in the
family could hear, "let this child be the Devil itself!"

This oath was fulfilled as she lay, delivering the
hexed baby. Thunder and lightning rattled in the
clouds over the Pine Barrens to the west and beaches

9

he east, and the newborn came into the world in an
earthly fury.

Mrs. Leeds recoiled in terror as the child she had
nned was horribly deformed. Instead of a cherubic
e, its head was elongated, and horns protruded from
skull.

Details of the earliest years in the Devil's life have
en lost in time, and there are questions regarding the
cts" surrounding its birth.

Some in the Garden State say it was a Mrs.
ourds, not Leeds, who is the creature's mother; some
y it was in Pleasantville, not Leeds Point, where the
rth took place.

What is certain is that the Jersey Devil has since
ade its heinous presence well known across South
rsey and into parts of three other states.

Scientists and pragmatists have dismissed the
ing as myth, or, as a stretch, a "marsupial carnivore
fissiped."

The Philadelphia Zoo once offered a $10,000
ward for the capture of the Devil. Perhaps, the offer
still valid.

Some rejected the very notion of a monster from
outh Jersey, calling it "idiocy." But monster or myth,
eports of its existence have persisted through the
enerations.

In their 1976 book, "The Jersey Devil," authors
ames F. McCloy and Roy Miller Jr. include maps
which plot the sightings of the Devil in its "flights"
across the region.

While reports of Jersey Devil sightings have been
plentiful in Atlantic, Gloucester, Ocean and Cape May
counties in New Jersey, the beast has also been spotted

BERKS THE BIZARRE

spotted as far north as Spring Valley, N.Y., and as west as Reading.

It was a "week of terror" in January, 1909, which the Jersey Devil went on a horrifying rampag

During that cold month, the grotesque beast s shivers up the spines of those in busy towns a remote rural areas alike as it scampered wildly on b sides of the Delaware River.

There was an eerie similarity in the descripti provided by eyewitnesses who were unfortun enough to be in the path of the wayward freak nature.

Although some said it resembled a "wing kangaroo," and others described it as a six-foot, ap shaped monstrosity with alligator skin, most agreed possessed a horse-like head atop a long, thin neck.

A spiny tail trailed behind its furry rump, and b wings gave it flight.

A shrill, cackling sound split the ears of those w heard the Jersey Devil, and those who sparked i anger shuddered as its bulging eyes turned red a glowing coals and fire shot out of its mouth.

Such is what one woman in the 1500 block Ellsworth Street in the heart of South Philadelph experienced as the Devil alighted in her back yard.

Up in Bristol, Buck County, the mutant being wa chased and even shot at by the borough police chief.

And in Reading, the Jersey Devil may hav appeared to a pair of police officers on routine patrol i the northeastern section of the city.

The incident received scant notice in the city o January 22, 1909, at precisely the time the creature wa making its swift and terrifying way from town to town

11

BERKS THE BIZARRE

Officers Weller and Reber were trudging through vly-fallen snow at 11th and Pike Streets when nething caught their eyes near the baseball field re.

It was the shadowy silhouette of an distinguishable animal. The patrolmen's first ughts were that it was a stray cow or horse.

As they walked toward the dark figure, intending round it up and remove it to a shelter, they were ken to the very roots of their sensibilities.

In their report to their superiors at the end of their ft, the officers declared that as they approached the ity, it vanished right in front of their eyes.

They swore they both had their eyes riveted to it they ambled toward it, fearing it may be spooked d bolt.

They were positive it did not run, did not fly, did t melt into the ground. It simply disappeared, into n air.

A report in the next day's newspaper alerted the izenry to the strange episode.

"As if to mock them," the dispatch said, "all ound them in the snow were hoof marks. Those, ey say, are all at one spot. There is no trail.

"The officers assert they are not superstitious, but e chasing of visions has them guessing!"

It is interesting to note that while the Jersey Devil as been variously described by those who have come contact with it, there is one constant.

In virtually every case when the beast left visible vidence of its visitations, it left behind hoof prints.

Could it be that on that cold, snowy January night 11th and Pike, those officers were tormented by the

12

BERKS THE BIZARRE

Jersey Devil itself?

Who is to ever know for certain?

It remains another unanswerable question in annals of Berks...the Bizarre!

BB

THE SEANCE

"If someone would have told me this, I would believe them. Absolutely not."

The Kutztown area woman shrugged and arch her eyebrows as she set the stage for the conversati we were about to have.

The words are hers. Who she is must rem confidential, as per the arrangements. "I'll tell you t story," she said, "as long as you don't use my name. I'd like to think I have a good standing in t community up here, and wouldn't want peop thinking I'm nuts."

Let us, then, call her Gloria.

The setting was a weatherbeaten farmhouse on winding road north of Kutztown. Crowded by ta trees and thick bushes, the home awaits restoration k Gloria. As it stands now, the imagination need k stretched only a tad to accommodate tales of ghos and hauntings inside the old place.

"Oh, yes," Gloria said. "This place is haunted.

"Actually, I was warned about it before I boug it. A friend of mine who professes to have psychi powers told me she 'read' the house after we ha looked at it together a few months before I mad settlement. She said it was filled with energy–som

13

BERKS THE BIZARRE

...d and some bad.

"Well, I'm an adventurous type, so that didn't ...her me a bit. I got the place cheap, and I'm fairly ...dy, so I looked forward to fixing it up."

Gloria shrugged again. Her green eyes darted ...ward as she measured the words: "Until I had my ...t encounter."

"It started simple enough, and early enough," she ...tinued. "Another friend and I were moving a ...ckload of small boxes and things in on my first day ...e, and we stacked about six or seven boxes up in ... middle of the entryway. We went back to the ...ck, and when we returned to the house with more ...ff, those boxes were no longer stacked up.

"As sure as I'm talking to you, those boxes were ...atly lined up down the hallway, one by one. Now ...t, the both of us knew, was absolutely impossible. ... had them stacked up, I believe four on the bottom ...d three on the top, and we knew it. We also knew ...t when we got back in, only a few minutes later, ...ey were all on the floor, in a straight row. My friend ...d I looked at each other in amazement, and a certain ...nount of fear.

"We looked around, figuring someone was ...aying a prank. Nobody was there. We pretended to ...smiss it. In fact, I blamed it on the energy, or the ...ost, my other friend had told me about. Little did I ...now how correct I may have been!

"That was it for a few days. In fact, it wasn't until ...got moved in and somewhat settled that other things ...arted to happen.

"Oh, I heard the normal sounds of an old and ...nfamiliar house. I figured the rattling in the attic was

14

a squirrel. The low and grumbling growling noise w
the wind or something. Or, at least I figured--ar
hoped.

"That grumbling sound was the most regul
thing. I would be sitting in the living room, and fro
somewhere in the cellar there would be this soun
One time I looked around down there, and I couldr
find anything that could have been making th
sound.

"I never liked the basement. It has a low ceilin
and every time I went down, I could have sworn I sa
shadows and felt that someone was staring over m
shoulder.

"Then, that psychic friend visited me. She ha
done some non-psychic research on the house, an
discovered that an old man had died there, and other
who had lived in the place swore they saw his ghost.

"I thought I wasn't easily spooked, but when sh
first told me this, I felt like just abandoning the plac
and leaving it to the ghost. Then, she calmed me dowr
by telling me it was a harmless ghost, just looking tc
cross over to the other side and be released. She
suggested we have a seance.

"She called it something else, but the goal was the
same. We would conjure up the energy, or the ghost,
and send it on its way. At that point, I treated the
whole thing like some sort of dog and pony show. I
dearly love my friend, but I'm not into that kind of
stuff.

"Well, to make a long story short, one evening we
got together, and this is where it gets unbelievable,
even for me--and I was there!

"Shortly after she started calling for the spirit to

ve a sign, the moaning sound I had heard so often
arted up. It got louder and seemed to actually rise
om the basement, up through the floor and into the
rlor.

"It was definitely the same sound I heard before,
it now I could tell that it was a human voice. I
stened very closely and I swear it was an old man
ying 'where, why, please, why, where... .'

"My friend quietly told the ghost, or whatever,
at it should seek the light and go there. Still, that
oice continued.   And then, it seemed as if the entire
om was flash-frozen. I mean, there was this freezing
ensation for about ten seconds.   My friend kept
alking and didn't seem to notice. I almost passed out.

"As quickly as the chill came, it disappeared.
Then, there seemed to be a flash of blue-green light. It
as like a blue flash bulb went off, but not quite as
right. As soon as that happened, the moaning sounds
nded.

"My friend leaned back on her chair and sighed.
She said it was probably over. The ghost had found
the way to the other side. I sat there, dazed, for a few
minutes. I mean, was this some sort of movie set, or
something? Of course, I knew it was all too real."

Gloria affirmed that there have been no icy chills,
no moaning sounds, no rattling in the attic, and
nothing else untoward in the intervening months
between that psychic exercise and today.

"A few months ago," she added, "I was talking
about the house with a neighbor. He told me he knew
the old man who passed away there. He said the
man's body was found in the basement!

"He also said the people who lived in the place

just after the old man died there claimed it wa
haunted. He laughed at that notion, though. He sai
he didn't believe in any of that ghost stuff.

"Just because he's my neighbor, I pretended t
agree with him. It took all I had to tell him my story!"

BB

TREASURE HUNTS

It wouldn't be entirely accurate to state that th
streets of Reading are paved with gold, but in 1860,
when contractors were excavating at what is now the
corner of N. 8th and N. 9th Streets, a trace of th
precious mineral was discovered.

Throughout the years, specks of gold have beer
found at various locations throughout Berks County.

In 1854, geologist G.H. Philips reported the
presence of gold on Endlich's farm in Alsace
Township, and commented that the specimens he
found were nearly as pure as those which led the
"forty-niners" to California five years before.

Eager prospectors did sink some shafts, but no
gold of any mining quantity was readily found.

At about that same time, rumors spread that gold
was discovered on the old Esterly farm, along the
Perkiomen Turnpike east of Reading. Again, men
excavated the site, but found nothing more than
copper. Even that was not of sufficient quality and
quantity to warrant further exploration.

Gold dust turned up in the iron ore mines in the
Hampden Heights slopes of Mount Penn, and on

BERKS THE BIZARRE

outh Mountain near Wernersville in the nineteenth entury, but again, not enough to spark a Berks ounty Gold Rush.

If any treasures were to emerge from the depths of erks County, they are more likely to come from man, ot nature.

Legend has long held that a notorious band of ories led by the Doane brothers of central ennsylvania buried a caché of some $100,000 in gold oins somewhere in the foothills between Wernersville nd Robesonia. To this day, the exact location of that uried treasure remains a mystery.

So, too, does the spot where another golden trove s stashed, somewhere near Monocacy.

While some historians have speculated that the Monocacy treasure was also secreted by the Doane gang, little is really known about who hid, how much they hid, and where they hid whatever it was they hid.

In the summer of 1901, locals descended on the farm of Charles Tracey, where an anonymous prospector and several helpers were hard at work digging into a cavern which opened about five feet beneath the surface of the ground.

It was in that cavern, the man believed, that the treasure would be found. "I will not tell how I gained knowledge of the buried treasure, neither will I talk about my plans," he said. "For a while we were unable to get the consent of the property owner to dig, but now that we have secured it, the way to the fortune seems clear."

Stories about a buried booty in the Monocacy area had persisted since after the Revolutionary War. Some claimed the money was in the form of silver,

18

BERKS THE BIZARRE

others said it was gold. Some said it was the ill-gotten gains of a band of rogues, others said it was wartime payroll and supply money, stashed in a safe place and forgotten.

To this day, the tales of untold treasures continue to circulate in the area. Occasionally, someone will follow the trails with a pick, a shovel, and a dream, seeking their fortunes.

BB

STONE WILLIE

He could be Michael Pohonski. Perhaps he is Pietro Buccieri. Maybe he is James Penn.

He might be James Murphy, or James Maypenny, or even John Powers.

Some say he came from Ireland, Poland, Italy or Wilkes-Barre.

He has been described as a petty thief, a murderer, a peasant and a nobleman.

His body was found in a gutter. He hanged himself in prison. He was murdered, and the crime is still unsolved. Take your choice.

He is one of the most enduring enigmas and endearing characters in the history of Berks County. He is dead, very dead.

Dead for nearly 100 years, he is nonetheless very much among us.

He is Stone Willie.

What is known about Willie is that his petrified remains lie on a slab at the Auman Funeral Home, 247

BERKS THE BIZARRE

Penn Street, Reading. Therein, the "Stone."

Where the "Willie" came from, and indeed where whoever he was came from is lost in the mists of time and legend.

The notion of a petrified corpse, a mummy, a man turned to stone, is the stuff of the tabloids. Berks Countians have grown up with him in their midst, and while noone can say for certain just who he really was, he has been "Willie" for generations.

Officially, he is James Penn. However, that was not his real name.

The setting was the grim confines of the old Berks County Prison. Its bulky stone walls and tower stood at the head of Penn Street, on the site of the present tennis and basketball courts in Penn's Common.

It was cold that Tuesday night, November 19, 1895. On a thin mattress in his cell, a man lay dying. He had told his captors his name was James Penn when he was arrested on October 7 in West Reading.

Contemporary reports theorized that Penn was one of several petty thugs who descended on Reading that fall to ply their pickpocketing and card sharp trades on unsuspecting firemen gathered in the city for the state firemen's convention.

Penn was first apprehended in late September, charged as drunk and disorderly, and tossed into the "drunk tank."

Released on October 5, Penn enjoyed one full day of freedom. On October 7, he ventured across the Schuylkill to the Morris Brown boarding house at 8 West Penn Avenue in West Reading.

There, he took off his shoes, stuck them in his

pocket, and proceeded to sneak from room to room, stealing any valuables he could stuff in his pockets.

At a little before five in the morning, in Lizzie Dietrich's room, Penn bungled the burglary. As Penn worked his misdeeds, he heard the chambermaid rustle in her sleep. He dove under her bed, shaking the mattress and awakening Miss Dietrich. As she opened her eyes, she noticed a man's feet scurrying under the bed.

Calmly, she rose from the bed, crept from the room, and locked the door behind her. Penn was trapped. She hurried next door to the Penn Milling Company office where she telephoned the police.

When officers James Young and John Gottschall arrived, they found a gold watch, a razor and a purse in Penn's pockets. The items were quickly identified as being purloined from boarders' rooms.

The lanky, 37-year old was taken to the prison and charged with larceny. He gave the name Penn, while Alderman Frank Clemson misspelled it "Pann" in the commitment book. His age was also initially reported as 27, but later corrected.

He claimed to be single, from New York City, and a saddler or harness maker by trade.

Upon his arrest, he told the police chief, "Well, you nabbed me dead this time, sure. I made a bad job of it, but then I have been playing in hard luck for some time."

Sleeping off a binge was one thing for Penn. Facing court action and serious time in jail was another. He did not take confinement well.

The night of his arrest, Penn knotted a handkerchief around his neck into a makeshift noose

and attempted to hang himself from the door of the cell.

His agony was not over, not by a long shot.

Prison doctor J.F. Feick was called in by warden H. John Kintzer to treat Penn for delirium tremens, a malady which sent Penn into wild fits of rage. He wrecked his bunk, rampaged within the tiny cubicle, and screamed for help in driving away the snakes he claimed were overrunning his cell.

For more than a month, Penn suffered these kinds of random attacks as he dried out.

As the weather grew colder, Penn's condition grew worse. Somewhere at the beginning of November, his cell mate, James Clark, recalled that James Penn told him he was not really James Penn.

It was a name made up in haste, and to shield his real family name from shame. He indicated that his brothers and sisters were somewhat prominent citizens of Brooklyn, but would say no more.

Shortly after 9:30 p.m., November 19, 1895, the real story of the mystery man died as *he* died. Dr. Feick reported to the prison board that Penn succumbed to acute uremia, a condition common to alcoholics. The man who once bragged to prison buddies that he could drink a quart of booze at one sitting, had lost his last gamble.

A man was dead. A legend was born.

The night of Penn's death, Warden Kintzer called in Theodore C. Auman Sr. to dispose of the body. As was the custom then, Penn was literally put on ice until next of kin would claim him.

Nobody would.

The first real hope of finding Penn's family came

BERKS THE BIZARRE

in a note from Clark, who related Penn's deathbed tales in a note to the warden.

In it, he said Penn had told him he had served in the Army, but was discharged because of corns or warts on the soles of his feet. Penn said his family came to the United States from Ireland when he was about 10 years old, and his father once operated a popular hotel in Waterford. Officials here did what they could to track down Clark's leads, but none was ever substantiated.

Folks from Philadelphia, Lebanon, and elsewhere thought they had found their missing kin in the presence of James Penn, but none could identify the body.

For weeks, the cadaver of the man known only as James Penn lay frozen in the Auman morgue, then at 34 N. 3rd Street. Valid attempts to find his family failed, while an interesting thought tumbled in Theodore Auman's mind.

A few years before, he was paging through a German medical book at a book store in Philadelphia when he came across a chemical compound which was being used as a meat preservative.

Auman had long envisioned a time when chemicals would be used as a "modern" method of embalming human bodies. In the medical book, he had the formula. What he did not have, was a body upon which to experiment.

When all seemed lost in the quest to find the real identity and survivors of "James Penn," Auman asked local and state authorities permission to apply his embalming fluid formula on the mystery man's body.

He was granted that permission, and in the name

BERKS THE BIZARRE

of science, plunged a needle in a vein of the corpse. The fluid filled his cells, and what could have been the first successful chemical embalming was a success. Very much of a success. Too much of a success.

James Penn was dead. Stone Willie was born.

THE DEAD BURGLAR.

His Picture as Taken at Auman's Morgue.

Herewith is presented a picture of the ~~dead~~ burglar who died in the Berks jail ...~~d~~...~~Wednesday~~ night. It was taken ...~~a been~~ taken to Un-

Auman's formula was on the mark, albeit a bit strong. The body took on a mummified state, and almost from the beginning, became a medical curiosity.

Sure enough, word spread quickly about Reading's man of stone. Somewhere amid a flurry of graphic, 19th century journalistic reports, he became "Little Willie," or "Stone Willie."

24

BERKS THE BIZARRE

This publicity widened the search for Willie's true identity.

It also served to deepen the mystery. He was not, as one Philadelphian had hoped, James Manypenny, a long-lost brother-in-law. He was not, as one prisoner claimed, James Murphy, a petty thief from Wilkes-Barre.

Or was he? On April 25, 1896, the embalmed body at Auman's was reported as having been buried. Family members from Wilkes-Barre had identified and claimed him, and received permission to have him buried in that northeastern Pennsylvania city. He was indeed James Murphy, and his family was quite well-known in Wilkes-Barre. And, the "petrified" remains were transported from Auman's to Wilkes-Barre for burial.

Then again, he may have been buried in Philadelphia, as yet another report "confirmed."

Records in Reading city hall indicated that Theodore C. Auman Sr. did receive permission to bury one "James Penn" shortly after his death on November 19, 1895. The records say he was interred in Philadelphia.

Yet, a space where the date of the burial was to be indicated is blank.

Just how deep is the Stone Willie mystery?

When Reading Eagle readers picked up their papers on June 19, 1901, they discovered in a front-page article that Stone Willie had been identified, and was soon to be given a proper burial. But in historical context, the revelation further skews the Stone Willie story.

On June 12, 1901, Stanislaus Laviduski, who

claimed to have come to Reading from Poland in search of his lost brother, strode into Auman's undertaking establishment to see if "Willie" was really his brother.

He had learned of the unclaimed body through the Polish Consulate, which had been contacted because the man had earlier, and quite confidently, been identified as one Michael Pohonski.

Stone Michael?

Perhaps.

With every ounce of confidence and credibility which could be afforded a reporter, the 1901 article claimed the corpse was that of an immigrant who was serving a two-year sentence in the Reading prison after assaulting another Polish immigrant with a knife. Convinced by other inmates that he would be executed at the end of his term, this "Michael Pohonski, prisoner No. 2891," made a noose from carpet yarn and hanged himself in his cell.

The report claimed that prison officials provided that identity to Auman when they turned the body over to the undertaker. It was then that the Polish Consul was advised of the death, and there was much speculation at the start of the search for his identity that Pohonski was a Polish nobleman whose family was banished after a political scandal.

Laviduski viewed the remains, but hesitated making a positive identification.

He said the age, build, and dark hair of the body seemed to fit that of his brother, but since he had not seen him in more than eight years, he was not certain.

The following week, another story made the front page. Two men who identified themselves as Paul

BERKS THE BIZARRE

Kolsun, Philadelphia; and E.J. Sebest, a Reading saloonkeeper, positively identified the body.

They wouldn't say who it was, however. Sebest said the deceased had frequented his tavern, and had many acquaintances in the city. In his statement, Sebest was vague. "No, I will not give his right name," he said. "He was known as Michael Pohonski. Let it go at that. He was from Biafcoves, Ungvar Magge, Austria-Hungary. He was a Slav, not a Polander, and worked at Eckert's Furnace.

"The man he stabbed was John Yakia, born in in Wilki Wites, Sarlamange, Austria-Hungary. No, he was not from rich parents, he was a country lad."

Confused? So was former Reading Times editor Dick (Old Pete) Peters, who attempted to nail down the identity of Stone Willie in a series of articles in 1954.

The following winter, Peters noted an article in *Front Page Detective* magazine which thrust Willie in a brighter, if not broader, national spotlight.

Author Thomas J. Kennedy claimed Willie was "The Killer Who Turned to Stone," and none other than Pietro Buccieri, a shoemaker who was executed at the old prison after being convicted of the murder of St. Joseph Hospital nurse, Sister Hildaberta, in 1892.

Kennedy further claimed that the murderer was at the hospital to undergo surgery as the result of a severe burn on his arm. And, official records indicated that after his hanging, Buccieri was never buried.

Peters' researched revealed that Stone Willie had no scarring whatsoever on his arms, and Buccieri was laid to rest June 30, 1893 in Reading.

The convoluted attempts to identify Stone Willie have proven totally fruitless.

BERKS THE BIZARRE

Nearly a century after James Penn, or whomever, died, his leathery corpse reposes in a dark corner of a Reading funeral home.

Some things *are* known about the man of stone. He was 37 years old at the time of his death, he was a Caucasian, and he is indeed, dead as a doornail!

BB

THE UGLY FACE

Even her best friends confided that Florence Shalter was somewhat of a cut-up.

The 14 year old Bernville girl had, as classmate Jennie Brobst described, "a lively disposition."

BERKS THE BIZARRE

Florence teased other girls at Bernville High School, and was known to disrupt class settings with her jovial attitude.

Being scolded and reprimanded was nothing new to Florence, but when her teacher, William M. Pflueger, doled out a punishment which seemed to him to fit the crime, the incident in the quiet rural Berks County school made national headlines.

On January 22, 1901, Florence was a particularly feisty mood, and as she was working out a math problem on the chalkboard, Mr. Pflueger asked her a question. She answered, but in the process drew the ire of the teacher, who accused her of "making an ugly face" at him.

She said she didn't, he said she did. Both strong-willed individuals refused to budge. Since the teacher held in his grip the teenager's privileges, he told Florence to stand up on a front desk and make another ugly face to the entire class.

She wouldn't. Incensed by her refusal, Mr. Pflueger made her sit in a front seat, and held her in from recess. "You'll sit there and have no recess," he insisted, "until you make an ugly face." She wouldn't.

The matter reached Jonathan and Sarah, Florence's parents, who met with her teacher. He explained to them his reasons for detaining the girl, but those reasons were not good enough for them. They took the case to the Bernville School Board, which supported the teacher's action.

Still not satisfied that their daughter's best interests were being served, they hired an attorney, Edward S. Kremp, to petition the Berks County Court

29

BERKS THE BIZARRE

on Florence's behalf.

Atty. Kremp claimed in his petition that depriving the girl of her twice-daily recess periods was "unreasonable, unjust, illegal, injurious...and is inflicted because of ill-will, hatred, malice and without cause."

Furthermore, the lawyer claimed that if Florence was kept in from recess, "it will be injurious to her health and cause irreparable injury to her."

Finally, he wrote, the teacher's demands that she "make an ugly face" as punishment was "holding her up to ridicule."

On March 11, 1901, Judge Ermentrout ruled swiftly that the matter was not within the court's jurisdiction. "If we had to pass on all manner of punishments inflicted by school teachers," he said, "the court would have nice time of it!"

Judge Ermentrout threw the matter back into the arms of the school board.

Attorney Kremp intercepted it and filed an immediate appeal. By that time, the "Make An Ugly Face" story from Berks County, Pa., was making news and opinion pages across America.

The Shalters were granted a new trial, and on March 22, the case was presented in the courtroom of Judge Endlich.

Testimony was offered by the plaintiff, the defendant, and several character witnesses. Unfortunately, Florence's character was apparently not without its flaws.

BB

BERKS THE BIZARRE

WITCHCRAFT HYSTERIA
IN BERKS COUNTY

Nearly two centuries after the notorious witchcraft hysteria of Salem, Massachusetts, a Greshville woman felt much the same pressure and prejudice.

Witchcraft was nothing new to Berks County in 1891. Throughout its history, this land of schpuks and hexerei has been home to many strange suspicions and superstitions, witchcraft and "powwowing" among them.

Powwowers walked a thin line between faith healer and witch doctor, according to some observers. Able to combine chants, herbs, potions and mutual faith between patient and powwower, these practitioners of folk medicine were common throughout Berks County for many decades.

To their faithful, they were anything but witches. Those who practiced the dark sciences, however, were to be treated with a wary eye.

Thirty year-old Mary Ruth became the victim of what was presumed to be false accusations of witchcraft when she was charged with magnetizing a nearby neighbor.

Yes, magnetizing!

The hills and valleys just west of Boyertown were a hotbed of gossip when busybodies thereabouts found out that Horace Boyer's wife was diagnosed as being magnetized. That's what a Reading doctor told the Boyers, and word spread quickly back around Greshville.

Worse, word quickly spread that Mary Ruth was somehow to blame. Mary Ruth, they said, was a witch, and had cast a spell on the Boyer woman.

"I have been unable to eat or sleep during the past few weeks on account of being blamed for the illness," Miss Ruth told a *Reading Eagle* reporter on July 4, 1891.

Mary lived with her older sister and brother in a small stone home in the middle of the woods just west of Greshville.

"My brother first told me of the rumor that I was suspected of having bewitched Mrs. Boyer," she continued.

Mary had left home in her mid-twenties to work as a maid in several upper-class Reading homes. She had recently returned to Greshville, and she felt the neighbors treated her with disdain because of her experience in the "big city."

She did have one experience which may have changed her life and contributed to the rumors she was a witch.

"While I was in Reading, a dream book was given to me to read and for amusement I tried one of the things referring to the moon, but I had no idea of injuring any neighbor," Mary said.

Her story becomes even more bizarre.

Mary said she visited a witch doctor in Reading and asked if she may have done any damage by tinkering with the dream book. He told her a neighbor of hers had been magnetized.

"He didn't say whether I did it or not," Mary said, through a constant flow of tears.

"He gave me medicine and after I had taken it, I must have lost my senses," she continued.

Whatever "medicine" was given was potent stuff. That night, Mary climbed out the attic window, down a grape arbor and set out alone, in the darkness, to nowhere in particular.

Where she wound up was some seven miles away. "I reached the Catholic church in Churchville, and was brought back by a man whom the priest told to drive me home in a carriage," she recalled.

Incidentally, when Mary was discovered at the church, she was buck naked. "They say that I disrobed while in church, and also that on another day I passed through Greshville at noon without much clothing on my body," Mary sobbed. "I feel very much ashamed, but I didn't know what I was doing."

Mary's 45-year old sister, Hannah, confirmed that the young woman had been out of sorts. "She was so wild that she threw the furniture out the windows and doors," Hannah said, "and once, I found her clothes lying on the floor, and upon looking out the window I saw her going down the road without any clothes."

As the random charges of witchcraft built in intensity, Mary grew even more anxious. More than anything, she feared whatever legal action which could have been taken against her.

"I was told that the penalty for witchcraft was $1,000 and that we would be sued and they would take away all the property my sister owned and leave us without a cent," she said.

Buckling under the pressure, Mary decided to visit Mr. and Mrs. Boyer and discuss the matter.

She chose to visit her neighbors at two in the morning.

Horace Boyer was not particularly thrilled with his nocturnal visitor. He had already addressed the "magnetism" of his wife, and a Reading physician told him that if she was indeed so inflicted, she would have to be, well, "demagnetized" or death could result.

Mrs. Boyer had been ill for about eight years. "She would become so violent at times that she tore her hair out, tore her clothing and wanted to jump out of the second story window," he recounted. "Something strange was working in her. Persons who had seen other persons afflicted with epilepsy said they had never seen anything like this case.

"I was advised to consult a certain Reading doctor. I did so, and after describing the symptoms to him, he said, 'Your wife is under a spell. She has been magnetized.'

BERKS THE BIZARRE

"By whom, I asked, and the doctor said he couldn't tell by whom," he concluded. In any case, his wife's symptoms eventually eased, and she seemed relatively normal within a few weeks.

Mr. Boyer said he pitied Mary Ruth for what he believed were unfair accusations against her.

"I don't know anything about witchery or magnetism," he said, "I am only glad my wife is well."

Mary Ruth also weathered the storm of accusations, but how she fared in her remaining years is a mystery which remains in the nether world that is Berks the Bizarre.

§§

TEMPERANCE COMES TO TOWN

It was a hot day, that Friday, August 23, 1901. A short, stout woman, handsomely dressed and sporting gold spectacles, stepped off the train in Reading.

She was on her way to a speaking engagement in Philadelphia after a few days of rest in Ephrata.

She poked around the depot newsstand and picked up a couple newspapers.

She was Carrie Nation, the tee-totalin' saloon smasher from Kansas, in Reading for a precious few minutes. A Reading Eagle reporter managed to ask her a few questions, and answer a few, as well.

"How many drinking places in town," she asked. "About 174," the reporter answered.

"And how many churches?"

"About 70," the Eagle scribe said.

"What?," exclaimed the reformer, "174 drinking places and only 70 churches? What are the church people doing? They need a stirring up, and you can tell them that I said so.

"I would like to tell you something," she continued, "but the time is too short."

Perhaps that was for the best!

35

BERKS THE BIZARRE
JEFFREY'S GHOST

She had grown accustomed to life without Vernon.

He died on a quiet Tuesday in June, 1988. Went peaceably, he did. Cancer, they said.

Kathryn was on her own. Her only son was a few blocks away from her little home in Reading's eastern suburbs. He visited often, but was busy getting on with his own new life as a husband.

"I remember the night well," Kathryn said. "I was watching a rerun of Bonanza and waiting for some eggs to boil."

She remembers the night well because it would be like no other in her 70 years. It would be the night she saw a ghost.

"I was wide awake," she continued, "and you must believe me, I do not drink, nor have I ever believed in spooks. That night, well, I guess that belief turned around altogether.

"I caught a glimpse of something out of the corner of my eye. At first, I thought it was a reflection or something. Then, I turned, and he was looking right at me.

"It was Vernon. No doubt about it," she said, a tear starting to well in her eye.

"Oh, at first, I guess I gasped and jumped in my seat a little. But within a split second, I settled down. He looked right at me, he did. It was real. It was too real. I mean, there was Vernon, my husband who had been dead four months!"

She acknowledged the skeptical air of the interviewer. "I know it's hard to believe," she

36

demanded, "but I know what I saw. I was not imagining it."

An intelligent woman who had left a proud career as a nurse behind her, Kathryn was convincing. What was to follow, however, would test even the most trusting listener.

"To make a long story short," Kathryn continued, "he said nothing. He smiled, started to wave, and seemed to fall backwards into a wall--and right through it. He just vanished.

"Well, he came back. It wasn't on any particular schedule or in any pattern. Nothing like under a full moon, or every Tuesday, he would just show up. Two or three times. Then, about that third time, he spoke.

"'Jeffrey,' he said. That was all. 'Jeffrey.' Now, I had known a couple of men named Jeffrey over the years, but I could not for the life of me figure out why this, this ghost of my husband would say the name. I mean, it really confused me. I lived with it for weeks, trying to figure it out. I though maybe I had misunderstood, but I knew he, or it, said 'Jeffrey.'

About three weeks after the "Jeffrey" incident, Kathryn received a visit from her son and daughter-in-law. They had good news. She was to become a grandmother.

"It was great," she recalled. "Now, I would have something else to occupy my mind. I had come to believe that maybe I really was imagining Vernon's return. But, of course, I knew I wasn't.

"Anyway, he hadn't come for many weeks. And, that 'Jeffrey' thing kept bugging me. Finally, the call came from my son. I was a grandmom!

"It was a boy. It was born premature, and had to

be incubated, but they felt it would be just fine. And then, I was nearly knocked off my seat. My boy told me they named their son Jeffrey.

"It shook me up. I mean, it isn't a common name these days, and it was too coincidental. I tried to shrug it off, but found it hard."

A day or so after the birth, Kathryn managed to steal some time from her son for a talk. In the course of the conversation, she figured, she would ask him how they came to name their boy Jeffrey.

"I came right out," she said. "I asked him where they got the name for the baby. He kind of stuttered and stammered. I could tell he was embarrassed or something.

"He said, ' Mom, you'll never believe this... ,'" Kathryn continued. "And I felt I knew what he was going to say after that.

"He said he had a vision of his father one night, and it spoke only one word, and that word was 'Jeffrey.' He kept saying that I wouldn't believe it, but I knew better. Eventually, I told him my story. We both described the same vision, with the same motions and that same one word it spoke. How, or why it happened, and I guess if it happened, was beyond our comprehension."

But the story did not end with that strange coincidence. It is not a happy ending.

"About two days after our talk," Kathryn said through quivering lips, "I was doing a crossword puzzle at the kitchen table when in the corner of my eye I saw Vernon once again.

"He looked at me. It was a milky, transparent figure, but I could make out his face. He looked at me and this time he said five words. Five words I wish I had never heard.

"The voice was Vernon's. It had a slight echo, but it was his voice. It said, 'Jeffrey is with me now.' Well, my eyes must have opened wide as saucers and a chill ran through my body.

"The figure dissipated slowly, and as I squinted to see its last, fading shapes, my entire body shook when I heard the telephone ring.

"It was my son, calling from the hospital. I knew what he was going to tell me. Little Jeffrey was dead.

BB

BERKS THE BIZARRE
THE GHOSTLY PIANO PLAYER

The tale of a ghostly piano player is a familiar motif in the region.

In a home in Stony Creek, the faint sound of piano music emanates from a corner of a room. Psychic investigations by individuals with no knowledge of the building's past inhabitants bore out the fact that a woman who once lived in that house had been a piano teacher and, in fact, passed away on a chair next to her beloved spinet.

It is believed the ethereal music which wafts through the room is the manifestation of the woman's spirit.

In the Lehigh County borough of Emmaus, not only the tinkling of ghostly ivories but the screechy sound of a piano bench being pushed to and from the instrument has been heard by several members of one family, and others who have visited their home. Again, it was determined through historical and psychic probing that a woman who had been an avid pianist died in the house, and that her specter continues to haunt the place.

An even more awe-inspiring tale is told by the resident of a home along Fritztown Road, near the Berks-Lancaster county line.

"Sometimes it's as if there's a tape playing," says the sole occupant of the house, whom we shall call Sally. "Other times," she continued, "the sound is very faint, and very difficult to hear."

Sally is talking about the sound of piano music which can be detected in what is now the dining room of her home. But in Sally's case, there's much more

BERKS THE BIZARRE

than just an ethereal melody.

"I moved in here about five years ago," Sally said in a recent interview. "I was on my own, and the price was right. I never really gave ghosts much thought at all, until about the third week I was here.

"I was alone that night, in my room doing some mending. I heard it plain as could be that time. Someone was playing piano downstairs. There was no doubt. It was clear, very clear. It was very pretty, too. It was some classical piece, I guess.

"You know, at first I didn't give it much thought, at least for the first few seconds. But then, very quickly, I reminded myself that the neighbors' houses were too far away for me to hear their pianos, if they had any; and I absolutely did not have any piano downstairs.

"Then, I didn't exactly know what to think or do. But, big brave me, I figured I'd better check this out. So, I quietly left my room and headed for the steps. Of course, when I took the first step down, the music stopped.

"Well, I told myself it was my imagination. The trouble is, I didn't believe myself!

"So there I was, dealing with the unknown, on my own. I made it through the night, and just about forgot about it in a couple days.

"Then, I saw some spooky movie on TV, and it reminded me of my experience. Heck, maybe I had a ghost in my house.

"I have a good friend who's really into that kind of stuff, and he says he has some psychic powers, so I invited him over to have a look, or whatever. Little did I know what would happen that time!"

41

BERKS THE BIZARRE

Sally paused as she took another swig of water and regrouped her thoughts.

"Anyway, my friend came over and I went out into the driveway to meet him as he got out of his car. Now please remember that I didn't really tell him anything about the piano music. I think I only told him that something odd had been happening in the house, and it might be the work of a ghost. I mean, I felt silly even saying that to him.

"It's really quiet around here, and it was very quiet that night. He pulled up toward the garage, I walked out, and he shut his car engine off. As he was getting out of the car, we both heard it--piano music, clear as a bell, was coming from the house. I told him then that it was the same thing I had heard before.

"Well, we walked toward the house, expecting the music to fade away or stop by the time we got there. But, it didn't.

"In fact, as we stepped onto the porch and walked toward the side door, we were distracted by something in the dining room window.

"We both looked in that window, stared for four or five seconds, and turned to face each other. His eyes were wide open, and I guess mine were, too. We both saw the vision of an older woman, sitting at a piano and playing away.

"She was facing us, but not looking at us. And, it all happened so fast that neither of us remembered if we saw her arms or fingers actually moving. All I remember was that she seemed to have very pretty hair, and the music--which continued as we watched her--was quite clear and nice.

"My friend and I opened the side door, and when

42

BERKS THE BIZARRE

we stepped inside, the music stopped. Of course, we cautiously sneaked over to the archway to look in the dining room. Just as we both already knew, there was no piano there, and certainly no ghostly woman. But you can't tell me she wasn't there just seconds before!"

Sally has never again seen the apparition. The sound of the piano can still be discerned on occasion, but the ghostly musician remains elusive.

"Every time I go by that window, especially at night, I look out the corner of my eye, almost hoping she'd be there again," Sally said.

"Maybe someday I'll learn more about this woman," she added. "At this point, I guess I just don't have enough nerve to look further into it. Maybe I'm afraid of what I might find out."

ß ß

THE EGG-SUCKING DOG

Some of the strangest stories on the underside of Berks County's history come from the animal kingdom. Some are funny, some sad. Some a tragic, some heroic.

Take, for example, Duke.

Around the turn of the century, old Duke could be found spending his mornings napping in George Heine's shoemaker shop at 152 Penn Street. The graceful, greyhound-windhound mix would while the time away on quiet mornings until the fire gong at the old Keystone Hook and Ladder Co. sounded.

Then, it was off like a shot to the fire station for

BERKS THE BIZARRE

Duke.

Duke's career as the darling of the Keystones had a rather inauspicious start. A rancher in Indiana had no use for the dog, and stashed him in a train car full of horses bound from the Hoosier State to Reading.

When the car was unloaded in the rail yards here, the scorned pup leaped and ran. He finally wandered into the fire station at 2nd and Penn, where fire driver Jonas Kiefer took personal charge of the mutt he named Duke.

They say Duke bolted to the truck room every time the fire bell rang, and was at the hooves of the horse as it sped to the fire scene. While the firefighters did their job, Duke watched from the basket of the truck.

When he wasn't napping or "helping" at a fire, Duke would amuse the chaps at the station with his special trick, turning somersaults.

And then, there's the tale of Solomon Helbert and the 7-foot long black snake up Shamrock, Longswamp Township way.

In the summer of 1900, Solomon spotted the long, fat snake snoozing in his back yard. It scared the old man so that he jumped to his feet from his lounge chair and ran.

That in itself was noteworthy, since Solomon hadn't been able to use his left leg since it was broken as the result of a wound he sustained in the Civil War. So sudden and powerful was his response to the reposing reptile that the bone apparently reset itself as he vaulted from his seat.

What Solomon Helbert discovered about the snake, however, was even more strange.

44

BERKS THE BIZARRE

For several weeks, his grandson, Willie Rice, had been staying with him. Almost every afternoon, the two-year old was given a nursing bottle filled with coffee as he played in the yard. Solomon would doze and daydream as Willie entertained himself.

Solomon recalled several instances when Willie would chuckle and call for him. "Look, grandpop, see here," the toddler would say. Grandpop would cast a quick glance Willie's way, and dismiss the boy's uttering as child's play.

As Solomon and Willie returned to the house at the end of the play day, the nursing bottle would be empty, but Willie would still be very thirsty.

After the initial shock of seeing the snake wore off, Solomon came to a couple conclusions.

The more he watched the slithering beast, the more he felt it was looking for the little boy who had gone back home to his parents.

Solomon was convinced that the snake had been Willie's playmate, and had grown fat and happy drinking coffee from the lad's bottle!

As the summer wound down and weeks passed since Willie was at his grandpop's house, the old man saw the snake from time to time. Each time, he lamented, the snake seemed thinner and thinner.

Finally, some of the best animal stories come from dusty old newspaper files from the days when local news "stringers" sent homey gossip in from every crossroads village in the county.

On March 7, 1905, as snow drifts made roads impassible in Berks County, there was much news to be savored by Eagle readers. In Moselem Springs, Samuel Braucher was suffering with a sore finger,

BERKS THE BIZARRE

caused by a pin. "The finger is inflamed and nearly twice its natural size," the article noted.

But the big story that day out in the hustings came from Shartlesville, and the public sale of Amos Lesher. A man named E.R. Wagner went into a shed to fetch a team of horses when one of the steeds turned against him and "bit him in the cheek and tore the skin and flesh clean off; also severing part of an ear."

BB

BERKS THE BIZARRE

STEAL A HORSE, LOSE AN EAR!

Should you have been walking the dusty streets of the town of Reading in the summer of 1783 and come across Christopher Painter, chances are you'd have recognized him.

He'd have been the chap with no ears.

Painter goes down in the history of early Reading as one of two unfortunate souls who received what was once the ultimate punishment doled out to convicted horse thieves.

The theft of a horse was a crime down the punishment pecking order only slightly behind treason and murder.

To say the sentenced meted out to Mr. Painter could be considered "cruel and inhumane" by modern standards would be an understatement.

The penalty for horse thievery was set down by

the government in an act approved on March 20, 1780.

Someone convicted of a first offense would "stand in the pillory for one hour and be publicly whipped 39 lashes and at the same time have his or her ears cut off."

Convicted of a second offense, the thief faced all of that, and as a further mark of dishonor, the rustler "shall be branded on the forehead in a plain and visible name with the letters 'H.T.' (Horse Thief)."

Painter received the maximum for his first arrest, as the court handed down the following instructions to the sheriff: "He shall be whipped with 39 lashes on his bare back, well laid on; have his ears nailed to the pillory for the space of one hour, pay a fine of 22 pounds, 10 shillings, make restitution to the prosecutor and discharge the cost of prosecution."

In the latter years of the 18th century, such public whippings were carried out, often with large crowds present, at what is now 5th and Penn Streets in Reading.

It was there that Christopher Painter was marked for life at 9 a.m., March 1, 1783, and where, three years later, another steed stealer also lost his ears, and had them nailed to the pillory for good measure.

Justice was not blind to gender back then, either.

Take the case of Mary Givin, who was convicted of theft in February, 1768. For her transgressions, she was given 15 lashes at the public pillory.

A couple months later, Margaret Jones bared her back and was subjected to 15 lashes.

A crime as relatively minor as purse snatching could result in as many as two dozen lashes.

BERKS THE BIZARRE

By 1795, the harsh penalty for horse thievery had been tempered, as the conviction of Christian Hollenbush in January of that year called for a fine of 10 pounds and two years in jail.

Hollenbush kept his ears.

BB

BERKS THE BIZARRE

SWEDES IN A SNIT!

This is not to sound flippant, or demean what must have been a volatile situation at the time, but a front page headline in the *Reading Daily Eagle* of Aug. 16, 1873, now seems so, well, *bizarre.*

"RIOTING SWEDES IN VIRGINSVILLE."

Yes, while they've since dropped the "s," it's our Virginville, Berks County.

Tranquil, peaceful, little Virginville!

And yes, Swedes rioted there on a Tuesday in August, 1873.

There were drawn pistols, thrown rocks, death threats and tension the likes of which that sleepy Greenwich Township village will, it is hoped, never experience again.

There were 11 Swedish immigrants in a work

BERKS THE BIZARRE

detail on the Berks County Railroad, all under the employ of contractor Foster, Conner and Company, and their boss was John Bloomster.

Early on the fateful day, Bloomster left Virginville somewhat surreptitiously.

He later said he went to Hamburg on business, but his underlings suspected that he was headed out to recruit new laborers and replace them.

When Bloomster returned to Virginville that afternoon, he was greeted by rather surly Swedes.

As they stood their ground at their boarding shanty, they confronted Bloomster with their concerns.

A baffled Bloomster failed to soothe their troubled minds, and the concern turned to anguish, and the anguish into violence.

The workers rejected their foreman's explanation and threatened to kill him on the spot.

As one of the men taunted him with a club and a fistful of stones, Bloomster fled for safety.

The situation grew more dour as another Swede drew a pistol and gave chase.

Bloomster ran to Simon Dreibelbis's hotel, where Mrs. Dreibelbis gave him sanctuary in the cellar.

The "rioters" tracked Bloomster to the hotel, and when they threatened to throw stones through the windows, beat the door down and even shoot their way in if they had to, Bloomster was forced to find a safer haven.

By that time, several men of the village had gathered at the blacksmith shop in the rear of the hotel.

Bloomster scurried out the back door of the hotel

BERKS THE BIZARRE

and sought refuge with what he hoped would be a more rational crowd.

Indeed, the villagers sided with Bloomster and held the Swedes at bay.

Cooler heads prevailed and the Swedes returned to their labors.

A ruffled, but relieved John Bloomster kept a low profile for the next few days.

On the next payday, he gratefully accepted his company's offer of a transfer to another job site far away from the seething Swedes...in Moselem.

BB

BERKS THE BIZARRE

THE LOVE POTION,
AND THE GOWN IN THE PRIVY

So you thought strange divorce settlements and tales of marital mayhem are products of a stress-driven 20th century society?

Think again!

His name was John Smith. Yes, John Smith.

She was Annie Smith. *Mrs.* John Smith.

They lived at 17 Franklin Street in West Reading, around the turn of the century. They had been married 23 years, but that marriage was headed for a screaming halt in divorce court.

Annie charged John with an eternal discretion: He had fallen in love with another woman.

How he fell in love, or at least how John Smith explained it to his wife, vaulted this story into the realm of the bizarre.

John said his mistress wooed him with a secret and very potent love potion. Once seduced by the sauce, Smith said, "I just couldn't help myself."

When Annie found out about her husband's wanderings, she pleaded with him to have the effects of the potion reversed, presumably by a local powwow doctor.

He refused to seek help.

So strong was the potion that John lost all love for his wife, and after several months of quarreling, he left home as Annie shouted out the door, "Go, and *starve!*"

BB

It was a happier ending for Mr. and Mrs. Marks

53

BERKS THE BIZARRE

High, who caused tongues to wag in March, 1901, after word of their particularly strange domestic squabble was made public.

Facing a Reading alderman, Mrs. High charged her husband with ripping up her wedding dress and tossing the tatters into the outhouse.

It all started when Mrs. High defied her hubby and attended the wedding of a friend. That friend, said Mrs. High, had been meddling in their affairs, and he specifically instructed his wife to avoid her, *and* the wedding.

Undaunted, Mrs. High attended the ceremony, wearing the dress she had worn at her own wedding less than a year before.

"When I returned home," she told the alderman, "my husband was very cross. After I had changed my dress, he tore out both sleeves and soon ruined it. I have put up with a great deal, but no woman will see her wedding dress treated so without rebelling."

Hurt and infuriated, she packed up her belongings the next day and went to live with relatives.

As the man and woman stood before him, the alderman sought an amicable solution.

Mr. High was apologetic, promising his wife he would take her to Penn Street, where she could buy any dress she chose as a replacement for the dress which had been plunked into the privy.

Mrs. High seemed suspicious at first, saying, "Yes, but no dress could have the same significance to me as the dress in which I was married."

As the alderman continued to soothe the couple's troubled minds, tensions eased. Mrs. High said she

BERKS THE BIZARRE

would drop her charges of desertion and bad treatment if her husband assured her of his sincerity.

At that, the man offered to "swear on a stack of Bibles" that he would treat her better and really take her on the shopping trip to Penn Street.

She smiled, he smiled, the alderman sighed, and the case was filed under B for Berks...the Bizarre!

BB

BERKS THE BIZARRE

JACK THE HUGGER

They say he did it three times. Each time, he did it in full view of the public as horrified witnesses gasped and unsuspecting victims shrieked and screamed.

When Reading police finally caught up with the culprit, he begged for mercy. He simply didn't know what he was doing, why he was doing it, and promised never to do it again.

History has lost his name, but legend, or at least the ledger of January 27, 1900, records him as "Jack the Hugger".

It was just after dusk that evening when "Jack" perpetrated his first crime on Penn Square.

The contemporary police report reveals, "A young man stepped up to a woman and threw his arms around her neck. She gave a scream, freed herself, and hurried off."

Under the watchful eyes of a Reading police officer, "Jack the Hugger" struck again.

Within minutes of the first "attack", the gent strolled up to another young woman and slung his arms around her. "She uttered a cry and wrested herself from his grasp," reported the trailing policeman.

After following him the breadth of the square, the officer was about to apprehend his prey when, as the report continued, "he threw his arms for the third time around the neck of another girl waiting for a car at 6th and Penn. She was greatly embarrassed and crossed the street to the other corner."

Having seen enough, the patrolman nabbed the hugger before he could impose his amorous embraces again.

Hauled off to city hall, "Jack" was called on the constabulary carpet where none other than the mayor himself was holding court.

Standing before His Honor and an assemblage of law enforcement types, the man, caught red-handed (red-armed?), stopped short of admitting his guilt.

He said he was a farmer, and was in Reading on business. While in the big city, he freely admitted, he had indulged at a corner pub. Perhaps, he more reluctantly said, he had *over*-indulged.

While he recognized the fact that a police officer had personally witnessed his transgressions, "Jack" said that if he had gone on the hugging spree, he remembered nothing about it.

After a lecture from the mayor, he promised he would be more careful in future visits to city taverns, and would never hug strangers on the street, ever again.

A compassionate mayor dismissed the case, and "Jack the Hugger" returned to his farm, a repentant man.

BB

BERKS THE BIZARRE

A GHOST
NEAR DAUBERVILLE

Should you be a passenger aboard a Blue Mountain and Reading Railroad train as it rumbles along the line between Mohrsville and Dauberville, keep an eye out for the eternal spirit of a beautiful young woman who has been wandering the canal and rail corridor there since her senseless murder in 1845.

The story has all the elements of a classic tale of tragedy and its frightening aftermath. The unsolved murder of a popular, young maiden, and the return of her ghost to forever haunt those unfortunate enough to cross its path.

The story of the murder of Adaline Baver, the

BERKS THE BIZARRE

discovery of her body face down in the mud of the old Schuylkill Canal just south of the Mohrsville Hotel, and one sighting of her ghost more than 30 years later, is chronicled in *Ghost Stories of Berks County, Book One.*

Since the publication of that story, in that book, additional information has surfaced, adding more fuel to the phantasmic fire which glows in that part of central Berks County.

To briefly review the story, Adaline Baver was a young woman who lived on a farm outside Leesport. "She was a beautiful girl, of amiable disposition, which sought never to offend, whose life was, under those circumstances and in life's morning, by the hand of a murderer taken away."

The words are from a contemporary newspaper account, and *"those circumstances"* were, indeed, as we like to say, *bizarre.*

Adaline was murdered along the canal, in what reports of the day say was in the vicinity of Heffner's Island, near the Irish Creek Bridge.

That would put it in the area just north of the present Dauberville Bridge, along the B.M. & R. Railroad right-of-way.

The identity of the murderer of Adaline Baver was never confirmed. The suspicion that her ghost, and perhaps the spirit of her killer, still haunt the area, has been aroused on several occasions.

The day Adaline's lifeless form was found face-down in the mud of the canal bank was described in lurid detail by Catherine Seaman, who had been at work in the tavern of the Mohrsville Hotel on October 14, 1845.

BERKS THE BIZARRE

She stepped outside to secure supplies from a shed and, in her words, "when I passed through the yard I heard sounds as though some person were moaning. I called the hostler's attention to the sounds and he gave it as his opinion that it came from the canal and was likely caused by fighting boatmen.

"The next morning, a deaf-mute tramp came up the railroad and tried to tell us by signs that a body was lying in the water down the road, but we could not understand him."

That vagabond could not get his message across, but soon after, some railroad laborers made the grisly discovery.

"We at once proceeded down the road to see whether we could not identify the body," Catherine Seaman recalled. "When we arrived on the scene, the corpse was still lying in the water near the breast of the mill dam."

With an umbrella borrowed from another onlooker, Catherine turned the body over enough so she could see the face.

"I discovered a gash in the young woman's throat. At the same time, I remarked that she looked like the girl whom I had seen in company with a young man in the neighborhood," she said.

It was later confirmed that Adaline Baver, that same girl, was the victim.

"She was considered the belle of the community," said Seaman. She lived in the family of Solomon Fisher, several miles from Mohrsville."

Investigators were convinced that Adaline's body had been transported to the canal side near Dauberville after she had been murdered farther

BERKS THE BIZARRE

upstream.

That news sent shivers down Catherine Seaman's spine. "The moans I had heard were her cries as the heartless murderer cut her throat," she shuddered.

It was later confirmed, through a trail of blood, that Adaline was killed just outside the hotel. It was theorized that the murderer dragged the body to its final resting place in an attempt to fool authorities into believing she had been struck by a train and drowned in the canal.

The slashed throat was, so to speak, a dead giveaway.

Police, constables and sheriff's deputies conducted a sweeping investigation, and suspects were rounded up. A Minersville man who was seen with Adaline earlier on the day she died was charged with the murder, but was found innocent.

The crime sparked much anguish in the community, and all leads and suspicions were checked, but the murder was never solved.

Strange occurrences followed in the wake of the slaying.

One young man was arrested because he had been a bit over-zealous in his accusations of another. A judge admonished the boy, saying he was free to think whatever he wished about the guilt of the other lad, but to do so publicly was a crime.

Then, several persons who may or may not have had a hand in the murder case died, some under mysterious circumstances, very suddenly.

Rumors circulated around Berks County that the killer was a man named Beissel, or Bessel, and he was killed in a railroad accident shortly after he allegedly murdered Adaline.

In time, the case was relegated to the realm of the unsolved, the unexplained, and the unnatural.

Catherine Seaman's involvement in the murder never really ended. What she had witnessed in mid-October stayed with her the rest of her life.

One incident which followed, however, was particularly disconcerting.

She recalled something that happened several years after the murder.

"Two of my boys were out 'coon hunting at night and came down the railroad about two o'clock in the morning," she said.

"When they got to a point several hundred yards below Mohrsville, one of them saw a white figure walking close beside him.

"His companion could not see anything, although his attention was called to it by his brother. The dog, however, seemed to see it for he kept close to the boys and appeared to be frightened. When they reached the point where the girl had been found, the apparition disappeared and the dog commenced to frisk and bark as though he felt very much relieved."

Could Catherine's boys have seen the ghost of Adaline Baver that night? If so, they would not have been the only ones who have.

James Daubley was a horse buyer from Montgomery County, and was on his way home, along the Centre Turnpike, on June 6, 1878.

With him on his carriage was a hired man named Henry Schmeck.

The pair was about to stop at the Mohrsville Hotel at about 10 p.m. when something happened

BERKS THE BIZARRE

which would strike fear in both men's souls.

"It was the worst night of my life," recalled Daubley. "I am fifty years old, and I don't believe in spooks, but if I live a *hundred* years I won't forget what happened."

Daubley was adamant that he was not a drinking man, was not seeing double that night, and was not imagining what took place.

Daubley and Schmeck were approaching the hotel when, as Daubley told a reporter, "my horse gave a start as a bright object skipped across the road in front of us.

"The object skipped like a sheep runs and suddenly it took a jump and leaped over a tree twenty feet high and disappeared. Suddenly across the meadow, I saw the same thing. It went up into the air twenty or thirty feet and then came down and whirled over the road again. Then, we heard low singing. It was a strange kind of singing, sadder than you hear at funerals."

Daubley said the lights and the sounds were not created by humans. There was no way, he assured the reporter, such phenomena could have been manufactured.

The worst was yet to come. At once, the bright object took the shape and form of a young girl.

"It had long hair, and was dressed all in white. The arms were bare, and with one of them extended, it pointed toward the black woods over the canal. Then, I heard these words come from her: 'They dragged me down...they dragged me down...my poor life was robbed...robbed when they murdered me.'

"Suddenly, it shot into the air, moaning, 'I

63

BERKS THE BIZARRE

come...I come...the hour is here.'"

Daubley said the ghost's last words crescendoed into a shriek as it disappeared over the trees and into the night sky.

There have been other reports of the sighting of Adaline Baver's ghost both where her killer (or killers) slashed her throat, and along the route her body was dragged before being dumped in the thick mud of the canal.

One is the story of Darius Smith and his frightening encounter with a ghostly, moaning woman in white who manifested mysteriously from a wooded plot along what is now the "old road" between Mohrsville and Shoemakersville.

We present the testimony of Mr. Smith, whose tale of a ghostly gambol was published in a July, 1878, issue of the Reading Eagle and was carried in several other newspapers across the country.

It was about nine o'clock at night when Darius Smith quit his hay making on a farm west of Leesport and began the long trek back to his Shoemakersville home.

He had just passed through Mohrsville when his attention was diverted by a strange sensation that seemed to embrace his entire being.

In an instant, there arose from a nearby meadow the faint image of a young woman.

What appeared to be a white gown draped from her spectral shoulders. Darius Smith's eyes were riveted to the improbable sight.

Was it his imagination, or was a blue flame slowly enveloping the pale figure?

Was it a mournful hymn or sobbing he heard

emanating from the ashen apparition?

Was the wraith slowly ascending and circling over him?

Were those steely eyes gazing back at him, or vacant sockets where eyes ought to be?

Already stunned, Smith was paralyzed by fear as the phantom began to speak.

"There! There!," the ghost urged as it pointed a slender finger toward a clump of underbrush.

"Near that log," the form uttered until its words were cut short. "Oh, my — !"

Smith's own words detailed what played out in the ensuing moments:

"I was unable to move even a hand. It motioned and beckoned me to come. I followed, and it led me to the place. There lay the log, all covered with fresh signs of blood.

"Coming in close proximity I now made sure that it was the form of a woman. Her features looked haggard and worn, as though having undergone a terrible ordeal.

"I could not do otherwise than follow, more staggering than walking, more dead than alive, through and over the river, which fortunately only reached to my knees, down the right bank to the railroad where a small hand truck was standing on the track.

"This had the marks of blood as though a body had been dragged over it. There she beckoned me to sit. I sat down and the specter rose five or six feet above ground.

"The truck now started, and we flew with lightning velocity.

"I rode a mile a minute with the ghost.

BERKS THE BIZARRE

"Suddenly, I came to a halt, from what cause I am still unable to say. We were beside a little pond. She now led the way down to the water, looking so worn that she crawled more than walked. Nearing the edge of the pond or small creek, that was almost hidden by the high growing grass and woods, she exclaimed: 'My God! My God! Here...here!...here!!'

"And with this strange sentence on her lips, she fell into the stream.

"I now seemed to realize more than ever my perilous position. Fright took the place of stupor, and I with the womanly form still in the water, being dripping wet, started on a dead run toward home. I ran as I never before ran for about two miles."

Smith wound up collapsing at the gate of a friend's house near Shoemakersville. After a good night's rest, he attempted to tell his story to his chum.

"After fully relating my experience and taking a light breakfast and a cup of tea, I started on to my home with a full determination never to travel that road again by night," he concluded.

As you cross the Dauberville Bridge, particularly at night, beware that just north of you, a sad and restless spirit may dwell.

As the train slowly ambles between Mohrsville and Leesport, also consider that the phantom form of Adaline Baver may well be strolling—or rolling at a mile a minute— along the tracks, in an eternal search for peace, or her next unaware visitor.

BB

BERKS THE BIZARRE

MARY, THE GHOST
OF OLD MAIN

How many among those who have spent their college years at Kutztown University have not heard of "Mary"?

The mere mention of the name in and around K.U. conjures up but one image: The Ghost of Old Main.

This "Mary" is an enduring mystery, a ghost said to wander the halls of the 1893-era building.

And, said *not* to.

BERKS THE BIZARRE

Nobody's really sure when the restless, hapless spirit of "Mary" was first spotted in the landmark campus building.

Every generation of students in recent decades has had its share of those who swear they've seen, felt, or heard the ghost.

Where Mary supposedly lived and died has been off limits to students for many years. Most recently, that fifth floor has served as an equipment storage area.

Her spectral impact has spread throughout the building, apparently.

What's more, while Mary's presence sends chills through the mortal souls of students in old Main, Mary herself may have a companion.

That's the opinion of Lorraine Warren, who with her husband, Ed, make up a renowned team of psychic researchers and self-proclaimed "ghost busters" out of Milford, Connecticut.

In a 1991 visit to Kutztown University, the Warrens determined that the notorious fifth floor is indeed inhabited by the ghost of a young woman, likely in her twenties. She is doomed to spend an eternity there, they claimed, because of some sort of guilt.

What's more, a second presence, that of an older woman, can be felt in a small room near the elevator doors of the fifth floor.

That younger spirit is, apparently, Mary. It is said she committed suicide in Old Main shortly after discovering that she was pregnant. Just how she killed herself is a matter of debate.

Since her death, presumably around the turn of

BERKS THE BIZARRE

the century, students have reported odd happenings in the big building.

Some are relatively simple: Rapid temperature changes, disembodied footsteps, dining utensils gliding across tables.

Some are more complex.

"I have actually seen the ghost," proclaimed Beth, a student from Philadelphia who lived in Old Main. "She was, well, sort of homely, and she had dusty blonde hair and was wearing a light blue robe. You may think I'm crazy--hell, I thought I was crazy-- but I know what I saw."

Beth, who preferred we not use her last name, was adamant. "I saw this, this *person* or whatever, first, and then I heard the stories. Funny thing, too, I saw her standing by the elevator door.

"I must tell you, I am into ghosts, and am a true believer. It is not the first time I saw something from the other side. Down home, I have often seen the ghost of an old man who used to live in my aunt's house. But please, don't think I'm some sort of weirdo. I put it all in perspective."

Beth heard about Mary after she told someone about her sighting. She heard Mary killed herself by hanging herself in Old Main, and heard that she became pregnant after having a one-night fling with a janitor.

"She seemed shy and withdrawing, and seemed to cower as I looked at her," Beth continued. "It was actually a rather pitiful sight, and not at all frightening."

Another version of the story includes a ghostly dog, said to have been with Mary when she killed

BERKS THE BIZARRE

herself. The howling of the dead dog can still be heard echoing through the long hallways of Old Main, they say.

Some incidents in Old Main dorm rooms really do defy any rational explanation. Take, for example, the time a student accidentally spilled water on her clock radio. She unplugged the radio and set it aside to dry. Moments later, the unplugged, non-battery backup radio started playing, loud and clear.

Or consider the water that flows freely from un-turned faucets; the mournful moaning sounds that seem to billow from the elevator shaft; or countless other incidents which catch the students of Old Main off guard on a regular basis.

Because the legend is so powerful and the alleged experiences so numerous, the university administration has taken note, and has done its best to downplay any notion of a haunting at Old Main.

The week before Halloween, 1991, William A. Yurvati, a library technician in the archives of the Rohrbach Library at K.U., presented a paper in which he hoped the ghost of Old Main would be put to rest.

His diligent work did tidy up some of the rough edges of the "Mary" story.

One version is that the girl hanged herself in, or threw herself down the elevator shaft in the late 1800s. Yurvati pointed out it would had to have been very late in the 1800s since the elevator was not installed until the 1899-1900 school year.

In addition to the pregnancy theory, it has been repeated that Mary's ghost haunts Old Main because she died in the building the day before she was to graduate. She remains earthbound, and Old Main-

70

BERKS THE BIZARRE

bound, in search of a diploma she was denied by death.

Poring through the records of what was then the Keystone State Normal School, Yurvati came across a find which could have been the very genesis of the "Mary" tales.

There *was* a Mary. Of course, there have been many Marys over the decades at K.U. But *this* Mary, this Mary S. Snyder, could well have been *the* Mary who had a reason to remain in Old Main.

In Mary Snyder's story, there is no janitor, no noose, no elevator shaft, no suicide.

Mary, age 22, came from Limekiln, Berks County, was one of the 100 members of the class of 1895. She had completed her studies in college, had successfully finished her final exams, and was looking forward to graduation day on June 27, 1895.

Shortly after completing her finals, Mary complained of pain. She retired to rest and prepare for her graduation.

In the middle of the night before what would have been a glorious day for Mary, she died. The cause of death was congestive heart failure, brought on by inflammatory rheumatism. The commencement exercises went on as planned, with the class members marching through town in an early morning rain and into the college chapel for the graduation program.

There was a pall over the ceremony, however, as class members had learned of Mary Snyder's death the day before.

Black crepe badges were made, and each member of the class wore one in mourning.   They pledged to keep wearing them for 30 days.

BERKS THE BIZARRE

"Her life as a student brought out a noble character," a notice in the *Normal Vidette* school newspaper said of Mary. "She was possessed of more than ordinary intelligence and made very good use of her time."

More poignantly, the article concluded, "She showed by her life that while she conscientiously attended to all her duties as a student, she did not live alone for this life. While we sadly mourn her departure, we yet have the blessed assurance that death to her meant eternal bliss."

In his conclusion, Yurvati stopped short of totally denying the ghost stories of Old Main.

"The true story of Mary's death appears to be the origin of the legend concerning ghostly happenings in Old Main," he said. "Although these facts do not support or debunk the proclaimed sightings of the Old Main ghost, they offer an explanation behind a legend that has persisted for many years.

"Perhaps the memory of her untimely death, perpetuated by the legend of Mary, the ghost of Old Main, serves to remind us of our own mortality and the value of living each day to the fullest."

BB

BERKS THE BIZARRE

THE DEVIL DID IT!

In days of old, it seems that when all else failed, when every other rational explanation was explored and abandoned, the Devil himself took the blame for everything from personal agony and anguish to strange natural and *super*natural phenomena.

One would not normally attach any supernatural, and certainly not demonic, qualities to the Blue Rocks. However, an ancient legend regarding the river of rocks just north of Lenhartsville does involve old Beelzebub himself.

BERKS THE BIZARRE

The ridge of mountains which forms Berks County's northern border was a mysterious, foreboding place to the area's earliest settlers.

It was a dark, deeply-forested frontier into which only the bold would venture. The natives of the land, pushed deep into the woods, were unpredictable. Hostile beasts lurked behind the massive boulders, within the caves, and amid the thick underbrush.

Those boulders, those caves, and the very mountain ridge itself were all the handiwork of the Devil, they said.

To the east of the Berks County line is a similar deposit of boulders, with similar origins.

Legend around Lehigh County parts is that Satan was once told by one of his minions that potatoes were particularly tasty.

Unfamiliar with potatoes, Lucifer asked for a description. He was told they were round and hard.

In a quest to gather and horde all the potatoes he could, the Devil scoured the countryside and picked up anything hard and round.

After he had gathered thousands of what he had thought were potatoes, he was informed by another of his subjects that what he had collected were not potatoes, but rocks.

In fits of anger, the Devil ripped open his sacks of bogus spuds and the rocks spilled, forming fields of boulders such as that at the Blue Rocks, and what the Lehigh Countians call the Devil's Potato Patch.

There are several more legends which are rooted in the land around the Blue Rocks.

There once was a severely deformed tree at the base of the rocks. Its trunk and branches were

74

BERKS THE BIZARRE

contorted in wretched crooks.

Folks around there used to say that when the first white settlers ventured toward the rocks, they found that very same tree to be straight and tall.

It was under the broad branches of the tree that several of the men from the area would gather to begin their hunts or "chew the fat."

Sometime in the 1780s, they said, the usual gang of locals was assembled at the tree shortly after the sun had set. As they discussed the matters of the day, the sylvan silence around them was shattered by a shriek.

It came from above. Their eyes were cast into the night sky, and together they saw it.

Across the ridge of the mountains, leaping over Spitzenberg, dancing atop Schneidbarik, a dragon soared. A long tail of fire trailed behind its bloated body.

It vanished over the tree line, somewhere in the vicinity of the Pinnacle. The shrieking sound died in a faint echo. The sky, turned red by the flaming dragon tail, was black and placid once again.

The dragon had done what it had done so many times before. It had wriggled out of its lair (called a *drachelechar*, or "dragon's cave" by the Pennsylvania Germans), taken flight, and soared in search of a fresh kill.

There is a deeper legend about the dragon, and a particular cave near Virginville which is still known as Dragon Cave.

It is said that two Indian lovers, forbidden to marry because of tribal differences, committed suicide in the cave.

According to the Indian legend, the spirits of the

75

BERKS THE BIZARRE

dead boy and girl manifest themselves as a fiery dragon which flies from the cave to the Pinnacle on the anniversary of the couple's death.

The men who had just witnessed such a flight may or may not have known of the Indian legend. More than likely, they cared not a whit as to what the dragon may be. They cared only that it had retreated to wherever fiery dragons go after scaring the breath out of them!

All was quiet again that night on the mountainside. The men went back to their discussions, no doubt rattled a bit by the unexpected intruder.

At once, the ground shook, the sky lit up, and the unmistakable roar of the dragon again rattled their eardrums. Again, the beast took wing!

This time, it flew not along the mountain crest, but toward them! Closer and closer it came. They could feel the heat of its flaming tail, and were shaken to the bone by its ungodly howl.

Fearing the dragon was swooping down to claim them as its next meal, they ran and hid behind giant boulders.

Its prey scattered and safe, the dragon fluttered its craggy wings and landed on the tree under which the men had just been.

With a crackling boom, that tree was split and bent into a gnarled and knotted tangle. It would remain that way for many years after the dragon had made it its perch.

BB

BERKS THE BIZARRE

RUN OUT OF TOWN ON A RAIL

It was not the best of days for John Zuber.
Not by any stretch of the imagination!
"Professor Zuber", they called him. He was the organist at St. John's Lutheran Church in Boyertown in 1892, and one day that spring, he must have felt his whole life had caved in around him.

The 31-year old man, described as handsome, refined, and popular in the Boyertown community, was a bit down and out when he left that town to seek employment in Reading.

Zuber looked at it as a short trip to better himself in the big city. The Boyertown rumor mill churned out tales that he and the choir's leading soprano, Della Wentzel, had left together.

77

BERKS THE BIZARRE

That rumor did not sit well with Zuber's wife, who was back in Boyertown with their two children.

The "short trip" extended past five months, and his return to his home town could not have been timed more poorly.

His wife refused to see him. Hoping to secure some much-needed funds, he looked up Daniel Brumbach, who owed him money for a cabinet organ he sold to him months before.

The problem was, Zuber's wife reclaimed the organ while he was away. She informed the buyer that the organ never really belonged to John Zuber, and he had no right to sell it. Brumbach was one organ and one down payment short, and was intent on settling the matter in court.

So, as Zuber was relaxing at a Boyertown tavern, a constable approached him and informed him that he was under arrest for selling the organ under false pretenses.

Zuber sought to make bail in Reading, but the constable refused to take him there.

The accused man then asked the lawman to take him to his father's house in Gilbertsville, where he might get the money to pay Brumbach and settle the matter amicably.

Somewhere around midnight, they made the ride to the neighboring town, but Zuber's father had no ready cash for bail or recompense.

It was one in the morning when a disconsolate John Zuber and the constable returned to Boyertown. Zuber remembered the night well.

"When we alighted from the buggy we were surrounded by probably 200 persons, including women and children.

"As it was dark, I couldn't see at all. I had never seen such a nuisance to Boyertown before.

"They hollered, 'HANG HIM...LYNCH HIM...TAR AND FEATHER HIM...RIDE HIM ON A RAIL!' I saw a number of persons having a long fence rail. How many had hold of the rail, I don't know.

"The rail was pushed between my legs, and directly they raised me upon it and rode me a short distance, amid the jeers and shouts and hurrahs and laughter of the crowd.

"While I was being taken by the constable about a square away to the lockup, the rail was run against my heels and legs, apparently in attempting to ride me on the rail again, but I was taken to the place in safety."

The harried and humiliated Zuber spent the night in the Boyertown lockup, and when he was awakened at six the next morning, he faced another incredible scene.

"Another crowd had gathered there, and they hooted and shouted, 'JUG HIM UP,' and I don't remember what else. As the train moved away, I could still hear them yelling and hurrahing."

It seemed the townsfolk felt there was good reason to harass Zuber. While they had no proof at the time, they summarily charged him with adultery and misconduct.

Zuber's little jaunt was not his first, they said. On at least one other occasion, he abandoned his wife and children and left town on undisclosed "business".

It was eventually determined that the gadabout church organist never did elope with the choir girl.

BERKS THE BIZARRE

But, his transgressions landed him back in jail, unable to raise bail, and unable to ever again show his face in Boyertown without the threat of being run out of town on a rail!

BB

Residents of the present-day Hampden Heights section of the city of Reading may be interested that they live in what was once known as Helltown.

A chap named John Hell was among the first to settle in that area. Hell built a log cabin in the area of what is now Hampden Blvd. and Marion Sts.

He built another, and around this first, crude settlement grew a tiny village which was named after its first developer, Mr. Hell.

BB

BERKS THE BIZARRE
HE LOVES ME,
HE LOVES ME NOT!

"What goes around, comes around" is a familiar phrase, and a Berks County court case in 1909 proved that for a Reading man, a series of unfulfilled promises and pledges to a young woman came back to haunt him, not psychologically but financially.

George A. Rogers was one of thousands of Reading men employed at the P & R railroad shops in town. In 1902, he was introduced to pretty, young Sara Beuchler.

Sara lived in Reading with her sister, Emma Emerich, and toiled as a telephone operator in the city.

From their introduction, it seemed to Sara that George Rogers was the man she would wed. In fact, she claimed that as their romance became more intense over several years, he assured her time after time that they would marry.

After five months of courting in early 1902, Rogers popped the question. Sara Beuchler declined his marriage proposal, but felt so strongly about him that she totally broke off a prior relationship with another man.

Rogers called the woman at least three times a week at first, and sent her a letter a day. Finally, on March 1, 1903, George and Sara became engaged. Sara promised she would be ready for a wedding in two years.

In good faith, Sara said, she remained true to George over the ensuing months and years. She followed an employment opportunity to Philadelphia, but the letters and phone calls continued.

Then, there were gifts. George gave her everything from an umbrella to a gold locket with his picture in it. His letters became more amorous.

...Love for my Sara, who is dearer to me than gold. I will risk my life for you. Oh, how glad I am with I am with you....my dear, sweet peach...I could not sleep on amount of thinking about you. I am always happy when I see you....(signed)...Darling.

Although he had worked at the Reading freight depot and then the locomotive shops, and she was living and working in the Philadelphia area, their long-distance romance was as strong as ever.

Or, at least Sara thought it was.

Whenever he could, George arranged a liaison at Sara's home. Whenever she could, she met him at her sister's house in Reading.

Sara was gradually filling a hope chest with almost $500 worth of dishes, doilies, comforters and clothing. She said there was even talk of buying a home.

And then, her dreams were shattered. On Labor Day, 1907, Sara and George spent a pleasant day together at Carsonia Park. They rode the rides, played the games, and cavorted as young lovers do at an amusement park.

On the ride home, George reassured Sara that their wedding was in the offing. He would be ready in perhaps a year, or better yet, by springtime.

Glowing with the glee of a bride to be, Sara continued to cherish the gifts he had given her and added to her household inventory.

Two days went by as Sara waited in her house in

BERKS THE BIZARRE

Philadelphia. A week, then two weeks, and then a month went by. Nary a letter or call from George was received. Sara's heart was slowly, painfully, breaking.

On November 17, 1907, Sara arranged a meeting with George through her sister in Reading. He refused.

Fate brought them together at Fifth and Washington Streets in downtown Reading. She insisted that they talk. He tried to avoid her, saying he had to be someplace in a few minutes. In his haste, he assured her he had nothing against her, but offered no reasons as to his abrupt breaking of their affair.

After that encounter in town, George and Sara never met, and never talked to one another again.

Until they met in court.

In a trial which attracted much attention in the area press, Sara Beuchler sued George Rogers for breach of promise of marriage, and sought damages of $5,000.

The details of what seemed to be a whirlwind romance were laid to bare in the courtroom. Rogers' letters were read, an accounting of the gifts he had heaped on her was given, and both parties gave their testimony.

For Rogers' part, the loving letters, the gifts, and the promises seemed a normal, and non-binding, course of courting.

The Reading man freely admitted he had met, taken walks and gone to Carsonia Park with, and sent many letter to Miss Beuchler. But that, he claimed, is where their dating ended.

"I never made any promise of marriage to her at any time, neither did I give her wedding presents," he told the judge and jury. "What I gave her were Christmas and Easter gifts, just an exchange of presents between us."

One of those gifts was a locket which Sara wore to the trial. She noted for all that in it was George Rogers' picture.

"As to that locket," Rogers said, "I sent it to her, but it never contained my picture, as far as I know."

When asked about the wordage in his love letters to Sara, he firmly said there was nothing improper, unusual, or obligatory in sending "love and kisses" in the mail to ladies.

Sara saw it otherwise.

"I had made special preparations for the happy event," she said, noting that she felt assured a wedding was in the offing, according to her beau's promises.

"Now, I have no parents to go to, because they are dead," she said. Then, of her five-year fling with Rogers the 34-year old woman sadly added, "I spent my best years loving him."

BB

BERKS THE BIZARRE
THE GREAT RADIO HOAX OF 1938

It was a busy time of year in Berks County.

It was the day before Halloween, 1938. Final preparations were being made for the official dedication of Daniel Boone Homestead as a Pennsylvania state historical park.

In the city of Reading, postal workers toiled to move the innards of the old post office at Fifth and Washington Streets to temporary quarters up the street in the Koller Building at 126 N. 5th. The operations would remain there until the old post office could be razed, and new one built.

Young and old were bracing for the annual Halloween Mummers Parade down Penn Street. City Council declared Reading's streets to be "officially haunted," and when the parade stepped off, some 5,000 marchers were viewed by an estimated 20,000 residents who lined the streets to leer and laugh at the marching units, bands, and floats.

On October 30, 1938, after the day's work or play was over, many Berks Countians settled in their homes and gathered around their radios.

A good number of people would turn to the Charlie McCarthy and Edgar Bergen show, while others twisted the dial to WCAU, the CBS affiliate in Philadelphia, for the broadcast of The Mercury Theater that night at eight.

The cast was led by Orson Welles, who at 23 was already one of radio's most impressive and respected performers. Each week, he and his cast would

BERKS THE BIZARRE

dramatize a popular novel or short story.

Berks County, and indeed the entire world, went about its business during that time. However, a very real sense of foreboding and tension was never far away.

Hitler and Naziism were on the move, and the entire world was emotionally charged. Threats of German attacks on American shores were imminent, and the nation braced for increased worldwide hostilities.

At eight o'clock, however, those tensions could be laid aside for an hour.

The broadcast opened with the introduction of Welles, and cast members who included Joseph Cotton and Agnes Moorehead.

Welles spoke first, giving the preface to the story which was about to unfold. Then, a charming announcer's voice came in, delivering a fake weather report which preceded a show, ostensibly sent live from a ballroom somewhere in New York.

The ballroom broadcast was really part of the play. During the musical interludes from the ballroom, a network announcer, played by one of the Mercury vocal thespians, "broke in" with a bulletin that astronomers in American observatories had noticed strange explosions on planet Mars.

Then, back to music.

After a minute or so of music, another bulletin, then music, then more bulletins.

As the bulletins increased in number, the situation increased in gravity. The most crushing blow to the listeners' psyche was the announcement that an object had crash-landed in a field near Grover's Mill,

BERKS THE BIZARRE

New Jersey.

Anyone who had tuned into the presentation just a minute late would have missed the opening statement.

In it, the CBS booth announcer plainly announced that the Mercury Theater was, that week, presenting a play written by Howard Koch, and adapted from H.G. Wells' "War of the Worlds".

Near the middle of the show, that same voice broke in, and said, "You are listening to a CBS presentation of Orson Welles' Mercury Theater..."

By the time of that station break, it was already too late.

Listeners were panicking. Putting two and two together, thousands realized that the mysterious object spotted by astronomers and the unknown craft which landed in a New Jersey farm field added up to an invasion of earth by Martians.

Grover's Mill, N.J., chosen at random by playwright Koch as the site for the Martian landing, was to be vaulted from obscurity to immortality in one evening.

The town of about 200 residents, near Princeton, was coincidentally the location of a summer home of Orson Welles' family in his younger years. Koch, looking for a landing spot for his "invaders", simply closed his eyes and pointed to a spot on a New Jersey road map. He pointed to Grover's Mill.

From the time the "thing", at first presumed to be a meteor, landed in the field near the Garden State hamlet, the situation grew worse. The bulletins became ominous as officials sought to investigate.

The object, to the shock of many scientists, police

officers and curious on-lookers, suddenly opened its cylindrical casing, and giant Martian monsters emerged.

Their first act of aggression was to eject a flaming ray that killed many men outright and wiped out the remote broadcast equipment which had been sent to the scene by CBS News.

After other encounters at Grover's Mill, the creatures from the Red Planet massed and swept across the New Jersey countryside, in the direction of New York City.

CBS News was somehow able to dispatch new equipment and personnel to the scene, and resumed its coverage from the scene of the devastation and death-dealing.

For 15 minutes, the Martians swept toward Gotham, with sound effects and superb acting making the broadcast fantasy so very believable. Soon, the music ended and CBS shifted to continual news coverage.

"Streets are jammed...Noise in crowds like New Years Eve in city...Wait a minute...

"Enemy now in sight above the Palisades...Five Great Machines...First one is crossing the river...I can see it from here, wading the Hudson like a man wading through a brook...

"A bulletin's handed me...Martian cylinders are falling all over the country...Seem to be timed and spaced...Now, the first machine reaches the shore...

"This is the end now..."

After a station break, Orson Welles, who portrayed a Princeton Observatory scientist who was an eyewitness to the landing, began a lengthy soliloquy which should have revealed the fact of the fiction.

By that time, though, half the nation was deep in prayer, soaked with tears, or fainted on the floor.

The United States of America was under attack. Not by Hitler, but by a foe even more horrible, the *Martians*!

In Reading, scores of Albright College students from New Jersey were terrorized. They packed their possessions to rush home. They would see if their homes were still intact, and if their families were still alive.

Telephone lines across Berks County, and up and down the East Coast, were a tangled mess of calls from relative to relative, friend to friend.

"Have they reached your town yet?"

"My God, this is the end of the world!"

Relatives from Western Pennsylvania called Berks County kin to see if they were safe. People from Reading called friends and relatives in New Jersey and New York with the same inquiries.

While talking over the telephone to Sgt. Walter Trumbore at City Hall, an unidentified woman fainted as the confused police officer heard the broadcast blaring from her radio in the background.

When he answered the phone at police headquarters, a frantic female voice exclaimed some garbled words. Before the officer could console the woman, *thump*--she had fainted!

At least one church service in Reading was interrupted by someone bursting into the sanctuary with the news that Martians had landed. At one downtown church, the minister got word of the disaster and led his congregation in a prayer for deliverance.

Mayor J. Henry Stump was called by his brother, Robert, from East Orange, N.J.. He told the Reading chief executive that all was well, at least for the time being, but he and his family were getting ready for a quick escape.

Many Berks Countians who heard the broadcast or received the news via a friend, still recall the unsurpassed panic that swept the region and the nation that night.

At the end of the broadcast, after the Martians had taken control of a battered, burning and beaten nation, Orson Welles offered parting words.

He explained that the program was, "The Mercury Theater's own radio version of dressing up in a sheet and jumping out of a bush and saying BOO!

"We couldn't soap all your windows and steal all your garden gates, so we did the next best thing. We annihilated the world before your very ears, and utterly destroyed the Columbia Broadcasting System.

"You will be relieved, I hope, to learn that we didn't mean it, and that both institutions are still open for business...and if your doorbell rings and nobody's there, that was no Martian...it's Halloween!"

As newspapers picked up the story of the world's greatest hoax, reporters discovered that the situation grew so tense that the Red Cross and the National Guard were actually put on alert that night.

A year after the American broadcast, the same show was presented on Peruvian radio. Again, people panicked, but the South Americans went one step farther. Upon learning that the broadcast was phony,

BERKS THE BIZARRE

and that they had been tricked, they set fire to, and completely destroyed, the Lima radio station studios!

Howard Koch took full blame for the realism of his play, but he and the radio actors would never fully understand how the show could have touched off such panic.

Psychologists began to study how so many people went berserk despite the reassurances during the program. They wondered why so many radio listeners did not choose to turn the dial and readily realize that there was no danger as they heard Edgar Bergen and his dummy friends cavorting on another station, *WHILE THE WORLD WAS BEING DESTROYED!*

BB

BERKS THE BIZARRE

TRY, TRY, TRY,
AND TRY AGAIN!

Pity poor Charles Hunt.

Despondent and desperate after the breakup of his marriage, the native of Belfast, Ireland and resident of Cleveland, Ohio, was in Reading in May, 1892 when, depending on how you look at it, luck either saved or doomed him.

Hoping to track down his estranged wife as she was visiting relatives at 931 Spruce Street, Hunt came to Reading.

He knocked on the door of his wife's aunt's

BERKS THE BIZARRE

house and first seemed to be in a conciliatory mood. He politely asked Mrs. Frank Loose if he could see his wife and their four children.

Mrs. Loose told him his wife was not interested in talking to him. He presented her an envelope filled with money, and asked her to give it to his wife. She declined the cash and asked him to leave.

At that, Hunt became enraged. He burst into the house, tossed the money on the floor and angrily embraced one of his children.

"This is the last time you'll see me alive," he shrieked, as he released the child and stormed out of the house.

To Mrs. Loose's shock, Hunt then drew a pen knife and wildly slashed his throat.

The blade was dull and small. He could do little damage.

The frustrated man, foiled in this apparent attempt at suicide, shouted that he would return with a gun, and do it right that next time.

He ran to a hardware store on South 9th Street, where the clerk refused to sell him a pistol.

He had better luck up the street, where he managed to buy a handgun, load it, and return to the Loose home.

Standing outside, he fired a shot at his head.
Nothing.
He fired again.
Nothing, again.
Realizing the gun was loaded with blanks, he pulled a loaded cartridge from his pocket, placed it in the gun, and stuck the gun in his mouth.

He looked toward the house in which his family

BERKS THE BIZARRE

was ensconced and mumbled.

He squeezed the trigger. His eyes clamped shut. He was about to end it all.

He pulled.

Bang!

The shot echoed in the city streets.

Nothing.

The recoil of the pistol sent the bullet careening through his cheek.

He tried again. This time, he pressed the barrel of the gun to his chest and thrust his head back.

He squeezed the trigger. His eyes clamped shut. This time, he would end it all.

He pulled.

Bang!

Nothing.

The gun apparently misfired, leaving only a black smudge and small burn mark on his clothing.

By that time, a fair-sized crowd had gathered to watch the fiasco.

Hunt hurled the gun to the sidewalk and started to flee the scene. From the throng, a Reading patrolman emerged and arrested him.

He was taken to the city hall lockup, where a physician declared his injuries to be slight. After a night's rest in the Reading Hospital, Hunt was discharged.

Authorities ascertained that Hunt had been drinking heavily since his separation, and felt that he never intended to actually kill himself.

In that, he succeeded.

BB

BERKS THE BIZARRE

SAMMY

"Sammy," she would say, her eyes bright and quizzical as befit her youth.

She would wait for her playmate, patiently biding her time in the bedroom of her parents' Exeter Township home in the early 1950s.

Sure enough, and almost on a daily basis, Sammy would drop by for sometimes a few minutes and sometimes a few hours of play time with the little girl.

The little girl is now grown, a successful woman

BERKS THE BIZARRE

who moves and shakes with the best of the movers
and shakers of the community.

Engaged in a highly responsible career and
tending to little girls of her own, she has left her own
childhood far behind.

Those days of sweet innocence are now
imprisoned in books of old photographs in her
parents' shelves, and in smidgens of memory which
occasionally come to the fore.

But forever, the memory of Sammy—the trusted
pal and playmate—will linger.

The woman, let us call her Janet, long ago lost
track of her old friend. She's not certain if she's still
living...or, for that matter, when or if she ever *was*
alive!

To Janet's mom and dad, Sammy was a make-
believe friend, an imaginary playmate, a fantasy.

To Janet, Sammy was all, too real.

It all started the first night Janet settled into her
new bedroom.

"My mom and dad had just bought the house,"
she recalled. "I was about five years old. I remember
that when we were looking at the place, I felt very
comfortable. We were only moving about two miles
away from where we had lived, so it wasn't like it was
another world. What few friends I had made in the
other area would still be schoolmates.

"Anyway, the new house was very large, and my
room was, too. I remember vividly that when I first set
foot in that room, I said, very plainly, 'Sammy.' It was
as if I was calling out to someone.

"I also remember my mom looking at me very
strangely, not quite understanding what I had said."

BERKS THE BIZARRE

Janet said she kept quiet after that first outburst, but an odd chain of events soon unfolded.

"That first night I had to spend in my new bedroom," she said, "I felt as if someone was there, looking at me. Funny thing, though, I wasn't scared. I remember my eyes darting around, and then calling out, 'Sammy,' once again.

"Then, as I recall, I dozed off. Mom and dad had come in to talk and maybe read a story, but when I was alone, I felt I was not alone, if you know what I mean.

"The next thing I can remember is a feeling of warmth that seemed to wake me up. Then, I looked around the room and stopped at the foot of my bed.

"Then, I saw Sammy!"

Janet paused, her eyebrows arched as if waiting for this reporter to accept her story.

Story accepted.

"Now, I hope you understand, I really could have had no idea what the word, 'Sammy,' could have meant, or who it could have been. But I just knew that when my eyes met that person who was standing at the foot of the bed, I was looking at Sammy.

"It was a woman, a young woman. Thinking back, it could have been a teen-aged girl. I remember her face as being, well, gentle. She seemed to have a bonnet or lacy hat on her head. Her head moved very slowly, sort of pivoting on her neck. Her eyes never met mine, they just kept shifting slowly and almost sadly from left to right.

"I remember that I almost whispered her name. As I did that, she seemed to perk up and look at me with a sideways glance."

Janet said she never felt threatened by the

BERKS THE BIZARRE

presence at the foot of the bed. She told her parents of the gentle countenance, but they dismissed it as a figment of her imagination. "They never once treated it seriously," she said.

Sammy became a fixture in Janet's room. "It was as if her very quiet, very comforting spirit was always there," she remembered. "I would often see her form, either at the foot of the bed, or sort of hovering near a window. I didn't know much about ghosts, and those sorts of things, at that time. I only knew that this poor girl seemed as if she wanted to talk, or play, but could not."

How Janet came to refer to the entity as "Sammy" is the icing on the psychic cake.

"Again, I had no idea who or what a 'Sammy' was at that young age. But we lived in that house for about five years. And, I can recall that at about the age of ten, when I was a little more aware of things, I was still seeing and talking to Sammy.

"Quite honestly, though, I don't remember her ever talking back to me. She was always more of a constant friend, seeming to nod approval and listen to my childhood woes.

"Then, one day, right before we were going to pack up to move to another new house, something very strange happened.

"I was in the front room with my parents and the two older folks who lived next door. They were talking about our move, our new house, and how they'd miss each other.

"Then, the lady next door said something that I have never forgotten."

Janet paused once again. She drew a breath,

BERKS THE BIZARRE

leaned back on her chair and stared this reporter straight in the eyes.

"The next door neighbor told my parents that they had become very fond of our family, and, as they said, especially 'little Janet.'

"They said they hadn't had much luck over the years with neighbors. They had only gotten to know us, and now we were leaving. But the situation was even worse with the previous neighbors.

"It turned out that those neighbors moved out after their daughter had died, of natural causes, in that house.

"Of course, we hadn't known that. Or, at least I assumed my parents hadn't.

"Anyway, they continued, telling us about how sad it was to watch the young girl—only in her teens, they said—deteriorate so slowly and then die.

"They told of how she'd get up enough energy to get out of bed and look out her bedroom window every once in a while toward their house. And, they told of how grief stricken the family was when she finally died in what was my bedroom.

"I guess I asked first: 'What was the girl's name?'

"I almost fainted when they told me: 'Samantha. But everyone called her Sammy!'"

BB

BERKS THE BIZARRE

GOOD DOG, BUFF

On one of the hillsides that frame the Oley Valley, Buff, a cute, furry dog, cavorts within the walls of an old home.

"Oh, he's a mongrel, a mutt–whatever," replied Buff's owner when asked to describe his special pal. "He's Heinz 57, I guess, but he's adorable."

Buff does all a dog does to establish himself as this man's best friend.

"He runs to greet me when I get home, he whimpers when somebody strange comes to the door, and he eats–boy, does he eat," said the sixtyish man who traded his tale for anonymity.

BERKS THE BIZARRE

Buff's been around the house since he was a puppy. "My brother's dog had a litter," the man explained, "and this one was the pick of it. I'll never forget the first time I saw him. He looked up with those big, black eyes and barked just a little–something like 'buff...buff.' That's how he got his name."

Good old Buff. Big-eyed, loyal, trusting and frisky Buff.

"There'll be nights when Buff will scamper across the upstairs hall, down the stairs, and up to his food bowl. The sound of him chomping away his food is quite a familiar sound to me," the gent said.

Did I mention that Buff also does a trick?

You see, for good old Buff to amble across the hall, down the steps–and for him to chomp at his chow takes one heck of a trick.

Good old Buff's been in doggie heaven for three years.

Buff is a good dog.

Buff is a dead dog.

If the gent in the Oley hills is to be believed–and there is no reason he should not–Buff's restless canine spirit continues to frolic in his old house.

"Please understand," the man continued, "that I've never actually *seen* Buff since he passed on. But, I've certainly felt his presence and heard him, too. I'm not the only one, either."

BB

BERKS THE BIZARRE

A GHOSTLY LOVE STORY

It could easily have been discounted as blinding love, an overactive memory, a flight of the imagination or pure fabrication.

Whatever, an incident in northern Berks County early in this century was recorded in the journal of a minister and reported in the newspapers of Reading.

Those who investigate the mysterious machinations of the human mind will find nothing unusual in the progression of psychical, psychological and psychic events. Even those who probe more reality-bound realms would probably admit that the phenomenon was at once baffling and commonplace.

The following case is typical of many which rattle the cages of comfort in which too many people are imprisoned.

BERKS THE BIZARRE

It was a sad day in Hamburg, that March 22, 1905.

Hundreds of friends, relatives and acquaintances of Dr. William Harris gathered at his old home on State Street and then at First Reformed Church, where funeral services for the popular gent were to be held.

Floral tributes abounded. The scents of roses and carnations colored and sweetened the somber atmosphere.

Harris was to buried next to his wife in Greenwood Cemetery.

Before the interment, the Rev. G.W. Gerhard would offer hope from the Scriptures and a eulogy from his heart.

The minister would also reveal to the attendees an incredible story told to him by Dr. Harris in the last days of his life.

"It was evident soon after the departure of Mrs. Harris, his companion, that he waned rapidly," Gerhard told the crowd.

"He told me that some time after Mrs. Harris' departure, there came at night an effulgent light, streaming down through the ceiling within six feet of where he was standing.

"In the midst of this white light appeared Mrs. Harris, beckoning to him.

"He said that he was perfectly at ease and not a tinge of fear crossed his mind. Then, tears flowed freely down his face.

"Since then, he seemed to be on the decline. A few weeks prior to his fatal illness, he came to my home, and before leaving said he was so lonely...oh, so lonely!

BERKS THE BIZARRE

"That corroding influence we call loneliness was gradually sapping his heart's life away, until at last the man with a brilliant life passed away."

BB

104

BERKS THE BIZARRE

NOW HE SAW HER,
NO HE DIDN'T

For Cliff, the workday ended as had so many before. He had laid down the tools of his toils and driven the tedious distance between the factory and his modest home in the hills of Albany Township.

Carol would be waiting in that home, supper warm and table set. She would greet her husband with a hug and a "how'd your day go" in a Rockwellian welcome.

Sure enough, Cliff steered his car off the main road and onto the long gravel driveway which led to the house.

His dwelling was about 50 yards straight ahead, visible through a canopy of maples. He had made this

BERKS THE BIZARRE

approach for some 20 years, and each time a certain warmth would wrap around him. He was *home*, and his beloved Carol was moments away.

On some occasions, Carol would venture onto the broad front porch of the house in anticipation of her husband's arrival.

That balmy autumn evening, Cliff peered ahead and indeed saw Carol standing on the porch, dressed in–of all things–a nightgown.

The pink nighty rustled in the slight breeze, and a smile seemed to radiate from Carol's face. Cliff recalled that his wife gave a slight wave as their eyes met. Then, as he was about to stop the car on the broad turnaround at the end of the lane, she turned abruptly and walked briskly into the house.

In all their years, Cliff had seen nothing like this before. This somewhat sensuous greeting confused him. It wasn't their anniversary, his birthday, or any special occasion he could recall. Just why Carol was so attired was perplexing.

Perhaps Carol was feeling unusually amorous or light-hearted. No matter, Cliff felt he may have been in for an interesting night!

He shut down the engine and crawled out of the car. Striding toward his house, many thoughts snapped through his mind. Nothing, however, could have prepared him for what was to unfold.

He bounded the three or four steps up to the porch and swept through the front door into the living room and turned the corner into the dining area. It was traditionally where Carol would offer her welcome home.

The dining room was empty. The table was bare.

BERKS THE BIZARRE

Not a meal was in sight.

Cliff was baffled. Something was out of kilter. But perhaps, he thought, Carol had something special planned. After all, she had seemed to tempt him with her scanty scurry on the porch. Maybe that was a tease of things to come.

He called her name. He peeked into the kitchen, in the living room. There was no response. He opened the cellar door and beckoned her again.

Silence.

Fear and fantasy dueled in his thoughts as he began to ascend the staircase to the upstairs bedrooms. As fantasy came to the fore, his calls softened. Through a grin of cautious expectancy he repeated her name.

Silence.

With some fantasy still alive in his brain, he eased the door open.

His eyes darted about the room until they focused on the bed.

There, Carol lay, curled as if asleep. Cliff smiled. His coy wife was playing with him. Feigning a tip-toed stalk of surprise, he approached Carol to "wake" her from her "sleep."

Carol was not asleep.

Carol was dead.

Her body was cold. There was no pulse. In an indescribable instant, Cliff knew that Carol had passed from this, and his life.

He dropped to his knees. This man, hardened from a childhood on a northern Berks farm and a manhood in an Allentown factory, grasped his dead wife's hand and cried.

107

BERKS THE BIZARRE

Consumed by grief for several minutes, Cliff soon knew what he had to do. He called a mortician, a minister, some relatives and friends, and prepared to work his way through the agonizing hours and days which lay ahead.

The first to arrive was a representative of the coroner's office who would pronounce the woman dead. As gently as could be, he told Cliff that his wife had probably passed away in her sleep, at least eight hours earlier.

Cliff accepted the information, comforted somewhat in that Carol had died in peace.

But then, his eyes fixed into a stare as he recalled the vision which had greeted him upon his arrival only minutes before.

He knew what he had seen. No one could tell him that he had not absolutely, positively, seen his wife–dressed in a nightgown–smiling and waving at him from the front porch.

Logic told him this could not have been. Carol died, it was reckoned, in early to mid-morning, and probably soon after the two of them enjoyed an unremarkable breakfast.

That was probably the last time Cliff had seen Carol alive.

What he saw on the porch that evening would remain in his memory forever as a ghostly mystery which he would never solve.

BB

BERKS THE BIZARRE

THE DEATH OF THE HAWK MOUNTAIN HERMIT

Tales of ghosts, the unexplained and the supernatural abound on and around Hawk Mountain.

The lofty region of northeastern Berks County is a wooded den of mystery and legend.

Dim lights where lights should not be; eerie sounds coming as if from nowhere; and unfathomable events which defy reason are not uncommon in this otherwise beautiful corner of the county.

This is the tale of one Matthias Berger–*der alt Modas*–the old hermit–of Hawk Mountain.

After arriving in the New World about 1850, the

BERKS THE BIZARRE

German Catholic built a crude cabin at Miller's Dam, near Drehersville.

As civilization crept in around him, he decided to abandon this homestead and find quieter diggings on the slope of the mountain we now call Hawk.

Out of a deep forest he cleared just enough land upon which to erect a tepee-like hut. He lived off the land and the meager earnings from odd jobs done at neighbors' properties.

His was the life of a monk.

And, this monk of the mountain was regarded as a friendly, pious man who occasionally welcomed visitors to share his freshly brewed Blue Mountain tea and partake of his religious teachings.

He was known to baptize young people in a nearby stream and offer informal sermons beneath a massive cross he built near his hut.

Although he kept to himself and preferred it that way, Matthias Berger was a gentle and peaceful man within his remote and tranquil hermitage.

Described in contemporary reports as short and possessed of a well-trimmed beard, Matthias would sometimes finagle rides to Reading, where he would worship in a Catholic church.

To his few confidants on the slopes of the mountain and in the valley below, he expressed the desire to be given a decent burial in a cemetery of a Catholic church after his passing.

The spring of 1890 brought with it a parched countryside in Berks County.

The area went weeks without rain, and the underbrush of the woods was kindling which any spark would ignite into a raging blaze.

BERKS THE BIZARRE

On June 25 of that year, Harry Mohl hiked through the dry woods under a stifling morning sun. He was seeking honeybees.

As he passed near Berger's clearing, he opted to drop by and visit the old hermit.

Mohl faced an unsettling sight.

Berger's straw mattress and feather pillow were savagely shredded.

Rainwater filled pots and kettles which surrounded the old man's cabin. Now, it hadn't rained in three weeks, so Mohl reckoned those utensils hadn't been tended for at least that long.

Matthias Berger was nowhere to be found.

Mohl made his way swiftly to the village of Molino, where he told the locals of the scene on the hill.

In turn, he learned that Berger had been at a local mill just about three weeks prior. It was apparently the last time he had been seen alive.

A search party ascended the mountain.

In the midday heat, men combed the rocks, the ledges and the tree stands, searching for "der alt Modas."

They hoped for the best.

They found the worst.

One of the searchers discovered Matthias face down on the rocks. His clothing had been rifled, all pockets pulled out. The birds of prey had already had their way with most of his flesh.

The evidence was perhaps circumstantial, but overwhelming.

Amateur investigators figured the hermit was attacked in his hut, chased by the intruders, and killed

111

BERKS THE BIZARRE

on the rocky ledge some two miles from his home.

The motive?

There were recurrent rumors that somewhere in his hovel, Matthias had secreted a small fortune in gold. Those who knew the man knew better.

The mystery of the murder of Matthias Berger was never solved.

The person or persons who beat him to death and left his corpse to rot on the rocks never came to justice.

His body was taken from the mountain and given a Christian burial at a Catholic church, just as he had desired.

And Matthias Berger, the enigmatic and ultimately tragic figure, is remembered as one of the enduring legends of the "Eck," or "corner" of Berks...the Bizarre!

BB

BERKS THE BIZARRE

GRAVEYARD TALES

Imagine you are walking past a graveyard. The sun has long since dropped below the horizon and an eerie glow is cast upon your pathway.

At once, you hear it. A low, sorrowful moan drifts from inside the stone walls of the cemetery.

Your attention is riveted to the source of the sound. Nervously, you turn your eyes toward the scary skyline of monuments and tombstones.

You know beyond all doubt that the low groan must be rationally explained. Corpses do not rise from their graves or writhe in audible agony. "Night of the Living Dead" was just a movie. "Thriller" was only a music video.

BERKS THE BIZARRE

Shadows have begun to cast confusing angles of darkness over the lay of the land of the dead. Your eyes are cruelly teased. Your heart pounds. Your flesh ripples with goose bumps.

Then, you see it. Before your very eyes, a winged figure atop the most prominent memorial seems to move. Slowly, it pivots upon its pedestal. It bows. It *moves!*

Your eyes are affixed to the horrifying sight. All reason, all that is right tells you this is not–this cannot be–happening.

But as the groans provide a subsiding soundtrack, the angelic statue indeed twists and bends, as if to release itself from its base shackles and descend–or ascend– in a motion which might surely be the spark of a fire of fear which would consume you and render you a resident, not an observer, of the land upon which you look.

As you measure your own sanity, as your senses try to reckon with all that is happening, all ceases to happen.

The moans cease. There is silence. The statue rights itself.

Still, your eyes gaze. You haven't blinked in minutes. The race of your pulse ebbs. Your chest rises and falls in a breath of relief.

What was sunset is now a deep dusk. You must continue on your appointed rounds. Somehow you must put this all behind you and go on. You shall never share this, this hallucination or whatever, with another mortal soul for fear of ridicule.

Years pass, and against all logic you retain the memory of that strange encounter. You read about one

BERKS THE BIZARRE

person, one collector of tales of the strange and supernatural, who might be a sympathetic repository.

You find that person. You reveal to him the account of the evening you shall never forget.

He listens. He takes notes. Your story is filed in the bulging cabinet which is Berks the Bizarre.

What you just read is not fiction or imaginary. It is the condensed testimony from someone who opted to remain anonymous whose moments of fear really did take place in a cemetery which shall also remain nameless.

Supernatural dramas in Berks County graveyards are not uncommon.

The stark cemetery next to the New Bethel Church in Albany is awash with legends. Renowned artist Ben Austrian rests in peace there, and the body of legendary Hawk Mountain murderer Matthias Schambacher also lies deep in the rich soil.

It is said that Schambacher's more restless spirit rises from its grave on occasion and wanders in various manifestations on and around the hillside layout.

On the northern fringe of Bernville is the Haag Cemetery. Notable within its confines is the monument to Civil War soldier George D. Fahrenbach.

Near that tall statue, a gray lady has been seen kneeling as if to sift through the blades of grass between the gravestones.

With a bonnet on her head and no discernible facial features beneath it, the forlorn figure has materialized and vanished before the eyes of more than one befuddled passerby.

Legend around Huff's Church has it that unsuspecting motorists may cross paths with a specter which walks and vaults the stone wall which fronts the scenic cemetery next to the sanctuary.

The ghost has been known to startle steeds in the days of horse and buggy and turn the heads of modern-day motorists.

Two walled, family cemeteries in the Oley Valley near Lobachsville harbor their own ghostly secrets. For many years, the phantom images of a young woman and a young man have been seen drifting across a road which divides the two plots.

Legend has it that the two were teenage lovers, left heartbroken for the rest of their lives when their rival families forbade their romance.

To this day, their spirits meet in an ethereal rendezvous on the neutral ground between the two family graveyards.

BB

There's a recurring legend around the Reading neighborhood of Millmont that the headless ghost of a man who was decapitated by a train some time ago still lurks in the area around the St. Bernardine Street Bridge.

From time to time, and particularly under a full moon, they say, the ghost can be seen walking along the tracks.

One witness of this visitation said that as a child, he was walking across the tracks one day on his way home, and was startled when he saw a white figure gliding along the tracks, coming his way. "He didn't have a head," the man said.

"I don't think I'll ever cross that bridge without thinking about what I saw that day. And I really did see it!"

BERKS THE BIZARRE

GHOSTLY COACHES
AND PHANTOM STEEDS

When only the silvery glow of a full moon illuminates the night, it is easy to imagine a ghostly horse and carriage rumbling along a narrow Berks County roadway.

There are, indeed, stretches of back roads and specific settings where phantom coaches and teams have been heard or seen rambling or stopping by.

We begin at a place where so many ghost tales begin, atop Hawk Mountain in Albany Township.

Although haunted by spirits of murderers and the murdered, a pitiful little girl and other strange

117

characters, the mountain may also echo with the slap of ethereal horses' hooves.

Not too long ago, a respected psychic visited the old Schambacher House on the mountain.

The building is haunted by several spirits, one of which is an eternal equestrian who made a dramatic imprint on the "reading" performed by the psychic inside the place.

"I see this man, riding on a horse," he said. "He is very young. The horse is galloping. The man has a hat on, what appears to be a uniform.

"I see this man stepping out front here and coming in. For what reason, I don't know."

The psychic reasoned that the "spiral energy" of this mysterious horseback rider may well be the base line of much of the spectral activity that takes place on Hawk Mountain–which he later proclaimed to be one of the most haunted areas he'd ever visited.

"There is a cry, because the events that took place are being attracted.

"It's not a curse, but things happen here because of this energy. There are disturbances...like a peg-leg walking...heavy walking...a horse galloping...a cry."

The investigator "saw" something which at once confounded and confirmed what may be the source of the supernatural activity on Hawk Mountain.

"It was violent. Someone was killed, and I can almost put you on the spot. The base line is that one of the members of the original building here died this death. And, they died violently here."

The presence of the rider permeates the atmosphere in front of the old tavern atop the mountain.

BERKS THE BIZARRE

"The person who dies is about 27 or 28 years old. I'd have to say that it was the same person I saw galloping on the horse."

What's more, in his vision, the psychic saw the individual who killed the young man. The murderer fled the house after the evil deed.

He mounted a horse, but just outside the front door of the place, a creature described in the seance as a "great white bird" flew in front of the escapee.

The horse reared up, threw its rider, and the man was killed.

"The person who killed the young man was never punished. The murder was discovered, but no one ever did anything about it. And strangely enough, both o them, one out of suffering and the other out of guilt, are still here."

Thus, two of the ghosts at Schambacher's are explained by the psychic.

At the Old Village Inn in Morgantown, Berks medium Terri Klemm says she saw a psychic image of a horse and carriage pull up to the front of the old hotel.

"The carriage was struck by lightning," she determined. "I feel that the horse fell into a ditch, and the passengers were killed. I also see a big tree coming down, hitting them. The horse had to be destroyed, too."

Could this event, seen through psychic eyes of Klemm, explain the ghostly patrons who have been seen by employees and patrons at the Old Village Inn–especially during or just after a storm?

"It could be," she said, "that on rainy nights, this does happen. The incident plays out, and it seems as if the spirits may keep on traveling, coming in here to an inn during the bad storm."

A legend at Charming Forge has a headless horseman galloping along the road that approaches the old ironmaster's mansion of the ancient forge.

It is the ghost of a young man who was returning to the "big house" after striking it rich in the California gold rush.

Laden with saddlebags gorged with gold, and anxious to reunite with his true love who lay waiting in the mansion, the rider spurred his steed as he galloped through the tiny village.

For some reason, the horse was spooked. It whinnied wildly, stopped abruptly, and flailed its forelegs.

The young man clasped the reins, trying with all his might to bring the horse to its senses.

In that flash of fear and confusion, the reins somehow wrapped around the rider's neck. With a sudden jolt, the leathery strand was pulled tight. The man's neck was snapped and broken.

So violent was the thrashing of the horse that the reins cut through the skin, muscle and bone, severing the man's head.

To this day, they say, the ghostly figure of a headless horseman can be seen and heard galloping on the road that approaches Charming Forge.

BB

BERKS THE BIZARRE
THE GHOST ON THE SWING

In her dozen years of life, Missy always had a certain fascination with ghosts.

It was a childhood thing many children share–a fascination fueled by pop-up books of spooky old mansions, cantankerous Caspers and eerie tales told in front of roaring campfires.

"I don't know that I *believed* in ghosts," Missy said in her parents' comfortable home in a suburb of a suburb on the north end of Reading.

"All those stories gave me chills," she admitted, "and I was always up for a good ghost story, especially at Halloween. But, I don't think I really believed that there are such things as ghosts."

Now, as she stands on the brink of her teen-age years, Missy has some unresolved anxieties regarding the notion of the supernatural.

"Well," she said, as if to question her own words, "I think I have seen a ghost."

Missy's mother sat by her side as she calmly, and with a demeanor belying her youth, recounted the events which took place in an early spring.

"It finally got nice enough for me to sit out on the back porch," she said. "I really like to sit out there and just watch the stuff that goes on in the back yard.

"I like to watch the birds, whatever animals come in and out, and sometimes I just sit there and watch the clouds, or the stars.

"One day, and it was early in the afternoon and still light, I was sitting there, looking out in the yard. I wasn't looking at anything in particular, but all of a sudden the swing set caught my eye.

BERKS THE BIZARRE

"There are two swings, a sort of tire swing, and a sliding board on the swing set. You have to believe me that the day was very still, and there really was no wind or any kind of breeze.

"That's why I thought it was really weird that one of the swings started going back and forth or up and down or whatever. It looked like there was somebody on it, but there wasn't.

"That really made me wonder. I looked to see if a bird or something might have been making it swing, but there were no birds nearby. Anyway, the swing just kept swinging."

Missy shook her head as she recalled the episode.

Her mother interjected an assurance that her daughter was never prone to exaggerate or concoct any stories.

"I just kept looking at the swing. It just kept going back and forth," she continued.

"Then, and this is really weird, it *stopped!*

"It seemed to stop quickly, as if someone was on it and decided to stop swinging. I guess you think I'm crazy, but I really am not making this up.

"Anyway, I just kept watching, and then I saw him."

Him?

"OK, this is the strangest. I looked next to the swing set and standing there was this, this little boy," she said.

"It all happened so fast, and I thought maybe I was seeing things. But there he was–some little boy. He was maybe a couple years younger than me, and I couldn't really tell you much more.

"I was too freaked to remember much. I guess he

122

BERKS THE BIZARRE

had jeans on, and maybe a tee shirt, but I couldn't say much more. Like I said, I figured he was a little younger than me."

Missy's mother stepped in again.

"I remember the day well," she said. "Missy came into the kitchen, and it was very obvious that something odd had happened. She told me the whole thing, just as she told you now.

"Of course, I *did* think she was seeing things. But, I looked outside. I saw nothing. Nobody."

Missy said she has kept an eye on the swing set from time to time, but has never again seen the unexplained swinging or the phantom boy.

Did she see a ghost that afternoon?

"Oh, I don't know. I would like to think it really was my imagination or something, but I'm not stupid.

"I don't see things, and I know what I saw that day. The only way I can explain it to you–and to myself–was that it was, well, a ghost!"

BB

BERKS THE BIZARRE
THE HANGING TREE

"Ever since I was a little boy, that tree was known around the neighborhood as the 'hanging tree'.

"I remember that whenever we rode our bikes past it, whatever we were talking about at the time stopped. We all sort of glanced at the tree, every one of us knowing about the story."

The words are from a man who, now at 45, is a respectable and responsible member of his community.

His name must remain undivulged because of his fear that he will be ridiculed. Likewise, the owner of the property upon which the "hanging tree" still stands has requested that its exact location not be revealed.

Both, however, swear that what you are about to read is true and can be documented.

"I know what happened–what really happened–I have some newspaper clippings," the gentleman continued.

"A man, who was only about as old as I am now, hanged himself on that tree we all called the hanging tree. The article didn't say he committed suicide, but everybody knew he did, and how he did it."

Simply stated, sometime after World War II, a 42-year old man draped a rope over a strong branch of an oak tree in his side yard, stood on a wooden dining room chair, affixed a noose around his neck and leaped from the chair.

Said to have been despondent over the triple-whammy of health, marital and financial burdens, the victim was found dead by his own wife about two hours after the deed.

BERKS THE BIZARRE

"The story was well known in the area," our contact affirmed. "It wasn't just us kids who called it the hanging tree. I think my parents were even a little suspicious about it."

But, this reporter was not called merely to hear and repeat a local legend.

The presence of the old oak and the tales it could tell were interesting, but when that "hanging tree" became a "*haunted* hanging tree", it took its place in the gruesome grove of Berks the Bizarre.

There were stories about a ghost that may not have lingered around the tree.

Most were, in this writer's vernacular, "they say" stories and retold by vague and vaporous "theys" who could never be identified or interviewed.

"They" said the old hanging tree was haunted by the specter of the suicide victim.

"We" needed more than "they" could provide.

So "we" went to the present owner of the property on which the old oak tree still grows.

One thick and craggy arm still stretches from its trunk, a chair and a body height from the ground.

It is the Hanging Tree.

The woman who lives in the house once occupied by the suicide victim has looked out her kitchen window for 20 years and, for 20 years, that vista has been consumed almost entirely by the old oak, which rises as a leafy mushroom cloud in her side yard.

"I know the story. I know the legend. And, if your next question is if there is a ghost there, the answer is yes," the woman said with only slight prompting from this inquirer.

She budgeted her words.

125

BERKS THE BIZARRE

"Every once in a while, I see it. I hear it. I feel it.

"First, I get some odd feeling that something is about to happen. It's something that's very hard to describe. Then, I hear a rustling sound at the tree. The odd thing about that is that even when it's winter, and there are no leaves on the tree, I hear that sound.

"Then, if I happen to, I look toward the tree, and there is a glow. I haven't told too many people about this, but I have seen a glow there. It's hard to describe, too. It's well, a grayish-bluish shaft of light, which seems to hover around the trunk of the tree.

"I wish I could tell you it looks like it's hanging from the branch the man hanged himself from, but it's not. It just seems to hover there, sometimes near that branch, sometimes quite a few feet away.

"And that's my story," she said.

As profound as that story may be, and as convinced as that woman may be, there are still some unanswered and perhaps unanswerable questions.

Is what she saw an apparition? And if it is, is it the ghostly image of the man who took his life on that tree nearly half a century ago?

"I wouldn't doubt that at all," said the man who initially related the legend.

"There was always something spooky, something scary, about that old tree. I've never seen what that lady saw, but if she really saw what she said she saw, I wouldn't doubt it at all that it was the ghost of that man."

The woman was a bit more convinced.

Again mincing no words, she concluded, "Do I *think* that's the ghost of the man who killed himself? No. I *know* it's his ghost. As long as it stays out there and doesn't bother me, I have no problem with it."

THE SKELETON'S SECRET

To the old timers around Bally, it is still known as *der Grabebarrick*, or Crow Hill.

It is one of many rises in the landscape thereabouts, and it is generally unremarkable.

Except, that is, for the fact that it is haunted by one of the most fearsome phantoms in Berks County folklore.

The soil on Crow Hill has always been strewn with stones and boulders, and less than inviting to agrarian endeavors.

Sometime in the last century, a landowner on the hill eked out a living working the land as best he could and supplementing that meager take with a shoemaker shop in an outbuilding.

In the large, stone house lived this farmer, his wife, and their eleven children. Unlike their neighbors in the lower and more fertile farmlands, this family lived in poverty. Their personal appearances and the condition of their property bore out that fact.

They had resided in the old house only a few weeks until a neighbor having his boots repaired told the family their place was haunted.

Haunted, he said, by the sounds of disembodied footsteps and the frightening skeletal specter of an old woman wearing a white robe.

The apparition made itself known to whomever

dared to sleep in one of the upstairs bedrooms.

It got to the point that nobody could gather enough bravery to spend a full night in the room.

More than one person confirmed that as they lay between wakefulness and sleep, they would hear the slow footsteps. As their eyes traced the source of the sound, the vision of the skeleton would emerge from the darkness.

The ghastly ghost would slowly prowl toward the bed, but stop just short.

There, it would hover briefly, cock its skull, and slowly vanish into the nocturnal void.

Those who had reported the presence said it appeared the skeleton was actually harmless, even somewhat pitiful, and perhaps attempting to speak or be spoken to.

Although space in the farmhouse was somewhat at a premium for the family of 13, no man, woman or child chose to bed down in the haunted room.

On a cold winter's night, an itinerant artist stopped by the farm seeking shelter and a meal in return for a caricature of a willing family member or a sketch of the house.

The farmer invited the artist to share their warmth. The only room in the house available for his comfort, however, was the haunted one.

After a filling meal and some exchange of conversation, the artist retired to his chamber.

The man lay, waiting for sleep to claim his senses. From the bottom of the steps, a clock chimed twelve times.

The artist rolled over on the bed, and as he did, he heard the footsteps which foretold the coming of the ghost.

He rubbed his eyes as a dim glow formed in the corner. It took a human shape. Soon, however, it became horrifyingly obvious that this was no ordinary, ethereal apparition.

The skull, the ribcage, the bony fingers, were all evident.

Out of reflex perhaps, fear to be certain, the artist stammered and muttered, "What do you want?"

The ghost had been hovering and wavering, and would soon vanish. But when the man spoke, the skeleton stood erect.

"For many years," it said in a voice which seemed to reach from somewhere beyond all reason, "I have waited for this moment, when someone among the living would ask me that question."

The artist sat petrified in his bed. He was listening to a *talking skeleton!*

It continued, "My spirit could find no rest or peace until I shared my secret with a man of flesh and blood."

Its *secret?* The mortal's curiosity was fired by the prospect of a skeleton's secret.

The spook backed away from the bed and beckoned the man. With a crooked forefinger, it pointed toward the staircase.

The man followed the robed wraith down the stairs to the kitchen hearth.

"In there," the ghost said, "you shall dig and find a fortune in gold."

If he hadn't been fully awake by now, the prospect of prospecting for an unexpected treasure brought him to his senses.

BERKS THE BIZARRE

"I buried the gold there years ago," the skeleton continued, "when my husband left to fight in the Civil War. He was killed in battle, and soon after I also died.

"I never had time on earth to reveal the location of the treasure. When I tried to share my secret with those who stayed in my old bedroom, they fled in fear. You were the first to acknowledge me. You shall be the first to find the fortune."

Sure enough, the man found a pick and shovel, followed the ghost's directions, and found a sturdy box filled with gold coins and jewelry.

As he ran his fingers through the bounty, he heard a faint voice saying "I will now find peace forever."

He looked up to thank the ghost for the unexpected good fortune, but it was slowly disappearing into the night, forever.

It is said the artist woke the farmer to tell him the tale and share in the treasure.

The farmer used his share to make necessary repairs to the property, bring his family to a decent style of life, and improve both his farm and shoemaker shop.

The artist was headed for the next town, where he would purchase a new suit of clothing and a comfortable house with a small studio.

Never after that night was the skeleton ghost of Crow Hill seen again.

BB

BERKS THE BIZARRE
CLOSE ENCOUNTERS OF THE BERKS KIND

The notion that other civilizations exist on other planets, and are intellectually and technologically advanced well enough to transport their beings to earth has fascinated and frightened mankind since the beginning of time.

Cave dwelling drawings and other primitive art and writing depict an interaction between earthlings and strange aliens. Records dating to the Pharaohs of ancient Egypt, some 3,400 years ago, include hieroglyphics which indicate flying objects with strange creatures aboard.

Crude renditions of what could be spacecrafts are confounding to those on both sides of the UFO fence.

In 593 B.C., the prophet Ezekiel claimed, in Chapter 1 of the Old Testament book which bears his name:

And I looked, and, behold, a whirlwind came out of the north, a great cloud, and a fire infolding itself, and a brightness was about it, and out of the midst thereof as the colour of amber, out of the midst of the fire.
Also out of the midst thereof came the likeness of four living creatures...Every one had four faces, and every one had four wings...Their appearance was like burning coals of fire, and like the appearance of lamps; it went up and down among the living creatures; and the fire was bright, and out of the fire went forth lightning.
And the living creatures ran and returned as the

131

BERKS THE BIZARRE

appearance of a flash of lightning.
Now as I beheld the living creatures, behold one
wheel upon the earth by the living creatures.

There are those who theorize that Ezekiel's testimony of creatures and the "wheel" was indeed a close encounter with extra terrestrials.

In 216 B.C., a Roman document recorded "things like ships seen in the sky".

The plot thickens with familiar claims:

•The U.S. government has covered up the crash of a space ship on July 2, 1947, and still has–frozen–the corpses of its occupants.

•U.S. Air Force and Navy pilots have almost routinely chased Unidentified Flying Objects and have been told to say nothing to anyone about their encounters.

•A secret textbook in use at the Air Force Academy admits that extra terrestrials have visited Earth at least five times in recorded history.

•American astronauts in space have reported space ships from other worlds, but have been ordered by NASA to say nothing about their sightings.

Before he became president, Georgia Governor Jimmy Carter filed an official report that he had spotted a UFO while on the way to a Lions Club meeting near Leary, Ga.

Entire societies, scholarly research groups and intellectual cults have been formed to mull over the mystery and urge the government to "come clean" and reveal what these organizations say is incontrovertible evidence that we have been, and continue to be, visited by aliens from distant planets.

Berks County has not been exempt from the UFO

phenomenon. In fact, if you took a map of the county and drew straight lines from Hamburg to Oley, Oley to Kutztown and Kutztown back to Hamburg, you would have within it what could be considered a veritable hotbed of UFO activity.

The earliest recorded "wave" of UFO sightings in the modern history of the United States came in 1896 and 1897.

Reports at the time told of peculiar metallic objects which soared and hovered, and sometimes landed in remote fields.

Primitive airships were already in the skies, and some of these sightings were attributed to these man-made, earth-made crafts.

Some so-called UFOlogists, however, believe these 19th century sightings were honest reports of spaceships from distant planets.

There were scattered incidents of the sightings of unexplainable aircraft by pilots and crewmen in World War II, but it is generally regarded that the "flying saucer" era was born at 2:59 p.m., June 24, 1947 when 31-year old pilot Kenneth Arnold spotted nine mysterious aircraft which "flipped and flashed" in the clear sky near Mt. Rainier, Washington.

"Saucer-like objects," he called them.

Headline writers had a field day!

Five years later, a veritable frenzy of flying saucer sightings took place in Berks County.

August 25, 1952: Herbert Long was coming home from his insurance office in Kutztown. He turned off Route 222 near Maxatawny and was driving north through a farm field.

As he came to the crest of a hill, he was shocked

to witness a saucer-shaped object hovering about 15 feet over the ground.

Long described the large disc more as a large serving tray with a cover, some 25 feet in diameter. There were portholes near the top of the ship, he said. Through them, he claimed to have seen lights and shadows.

Between the domed top of the craft and a lower platform was a revolving ring which seemed to have pipes or antennae extending from it. Another antenna could be seen rising from the top of the dome.

For about five minutes, Long watched the craft hover. "Then," he told a reporter, "there was a terrific whooshing noise and the saucer left a trail of dark smoke."

"I could have hit the saucer with a rock," he recalled, "but I didn't move. The short time I sat there seemed like an hour. I was sure hoping someone else would come along and see this thing just as I did. I would have given my right arm for a camera."

Long's story shared the bottom of page one of the *Reading Eagle* with the report that Metropolitan Edison Co. (then known as MECO) had broken ground for a new, $2.5 million operating headquarters on the Pottsville Pike.

August 26, 1952: While the world watched as Communists threatened to take over Iran and Americans followed the campaigns of Eisenhower and Stevenson, Berks Countians were enthralled by an even more sensational event.

An incredible rendering by *Eagle* artist LeRoy Gensemer dominated page one and accompanied the story of Fred and Nora Snyder, who were the latest

BERKS THE BIZARRE

witnesses to untoward events in the skies over Berks.

The Snyders were in their Walnut Street, Fleetwood, home when, for some inexplicable reason, Fred awakened at about 2 a.m.

As the 65-year old Snyder looked out the window to check the weather, he saw something in the sky. "It was like a yellow ball of light," he said, "like the light of a coal oil light. I knew it wasn't an airplane."

Startled and confused, Fred shook his wife out of her sleep. "We both watched it. It made a wide right turn and headed toward Kutztown."

There was no noise from the street, or from the sky. There was also no fear. "If there are such things as flying saucers," Snyder deadpanned, "I guess that was one of them."

The city newspaper office buzzed with additional reports of UFO sightings throughout the county.

At the Kutztown sewage treatment plant, worker Fred Arndt said he, too, saw a strange light in the sky at about the time the Snyders made their sighting.

Mary Kerr, 17, and Carol Hauch, 15, were working at the Kutztown Swimming Pool later that day when they say they saw a mystery aircraft soar over their heads.

Cotton Street resident Carl Schurma, himself a private pilot, said he saw two mysterious yellow lights in the sky as he was driving his car on Lancaster Avenue.

The attending publicity also brought out Kutztown R.D. 1 resident John Mittl, who revealed four photographs of mysterious objects he saw at his mother's farm near Kutztown.

Mittl had the opportunity to grab his camera and

shoot the four pictures as the round object circled over him, turned abruptly and shot out of sight.

The 22-year old was actually heading for a wooded area to photograph wildlife when, in his words, "The saucer, or whatever it was, came straight down for some distance, made a sharp turn toward the east and then started to rise. It disappeared in a few seconds."

There was no sound, and because Mittl was observing the objects through his viewfinder, he could not provide a detailed description.

When probed on the matter, however, he did affirm that the object was not an airplane or a weather balloon. "I'm sure I wasn't just seeing things that weren't there," he added, "and the camera wasn't seeing things, either."

That August, Berks Countians kept their eyes in the skies, and the slightest anomaly in the atmosphere would result in mild panic.

A searchlight from the Wernersville Fireman's Carnival created a hazy image in the night sky when it illuminated a disc-shaped cloud just west of Reading. The press and police were inundated with reports of yet another "UFO" in their midst.

Then, on August 27, as Berks Countians learned their new Berks Heim would soon open and replace the old almshouse in Cumru Township, they also learned that at least one man might offer an explanation for the recent rash of flying saucer sightings.

Harry Feinauer, a 43-year old who studied silhouettes of airplanes during his World War II service, claimed to have an above-average knowledge of jet and propeller aircraft.

BERKS THE BIZARRE

The Birdsboro R.D. 2 man told a reporter that he had witnessed a most unusual sight in the sky near Birdsboro the morning Herbert Long claimed he saw the "serving tray" near Maxatawny.

Feinauer said he saw a four-engine jet flying high, and something quite odd discharged from it.

"At first I thought a wing had fallen off the plane," he stated.

"The small object was the shape of a clam and the color of aluminum. It must have dropped several hundred feet before it zig-zagged sharply and disappeared from sight very quickly."

While he avowed an awareness of the appearances of most American planes, he admitted the craft was unlike any other he had ever seen.

"Maybe it was one of our planes," he said, "and then again, maybe it wasn't. I don't believe in jumping to conclusions."

Air National Guard officials at Reading Airport soft-pedaled the UFO reports, offering that the presence of long vapor trails left by a 10-engine B-36 inter-continental bomber and a nearby jet fighter may have had something to do with the sightings.

Berks Countians were not alone, as much of the nation marveled at bizarre lights and crafts.

Hundreds of UFO sightings were reported to authorities across the United States in the summer of 1952.

People Today magazine speculated that the "flying saucers" were actually experimental and secret missiles and airplanes from within the U.S. and Russian air forces.

Of course, it *was* a time of high anxiety as the

137

BERKS THE BIZARRE

Cold War was raging and suspicions were mounting on both sides of the Iron Curtain as to what kind of lethal weapons each side possessed.

Army Secretary Frank Pace flatly denied that the alleged "saucers" were secret weapons from either side. As well, the secretary said he believed the sightings of unexplainable aircraft were products of fertile imaginations.

He told a reporter, "We have enough real problems to worry about without conjuring up imaginary ones."

Although there were isolated reports of UFO sightings in Berks over the next decade and a half, it was not until 1967 that another noticeable bunching of incidents took place.

In March, a Sixth Ward resident called the Reading fire department to report a UFO which was making a peculiar whirring sound and discharging fiery items.

The report was dismissed by officials as an F27 turboprop airplane on approach to Reading Airport in the fog.

In neighboring Schuylkill County, an Auburn funeral director said she witnessed a daylight appearance of a "flying saucer" on a back road between Schuylkill Haven and Auburn.

Mrs. George Binner said the flying object was shaped somewhat like a football, was green in color, and had chrome bands wrapped around it.

For about three minutes, the craft hovered over the road at treetop level before it zoomed quickly and silently over a northern hill.

In late June, 1967, many Readingites witnessed a

BERKS THE BIZARRE

blue-green object with a red dot in the middle hovering some 300 feet over Lancaster Avenue. No explanation was given.

Then, on June 3, Kathleen and Richard Vollenwieder of the Oley Valley saw what they could best describe as, well, a flying saucer, as they returned home at about 1 a.m.

"My wife turned to me and her mouth dropped and she said, 'Look behind you,'" Vollenwieder told investigators.

The chemist and his registered nurse wife then both witnessed a yellow-orange saucer soar, emitting a red light which blinked every ten seconds.

"Sometimes it went up and down and varied its speed and once it dipped behind the hills for an instant, as if it were studying something," he continued.

Vollenwieder discounted any notions that the object was an airplane or helicopter.

After the initial publicity appeared in the *Reading Times*, Carmelo Cataldi of Kutztown notified the press that he, too, had seen the object.

Cataldi said the craft lingered in his area for about 45 minutes before shooting off toward Hamburg.

It was there that Hamburg Police Chief Charles Miller confirmed that he watched the saucer along with several others.

Cynics at the FAA tower at the Reading Airport said there was no doubt that something unusual was in the sky that night, but it was nothing more than the Goodyear blimp.

Not so, said Goodyear. Yes, one of the blimps was crossing Pennsylvania that weekend, but was almost positively *not* in that area at that time. In fact, the closest the airship could have come to Hamburg on the cross-Commonwealth transit would have been some 20 miles to the north.

UFO hysteria in the county seemed to languish for several years following that spate of sightings.

In 1973, however, it came back—with a vengeance!

Sharyn Semmel, eight months pregnant and with a three-year old at the time, was a registered nurse and a confirmed non-believer in "Men from Mars".

But, an incident near her Hamburg area home on March 12, 1973, shook her to her roots and was the first of more than a dozen UFO sightings in the "Berks Triangle" in the next two months.

Mrs. Semmel was returning home along Focht Lane in her Ford Pinto at about 10:30 at night when her young son tugged at her and said, "Mommy, what's that?"

She looked up to see a bizarre object with throbbing red lights in front and white lights in the rear. The confused mother could not answer her son. She sat agape, her heart pounded, and she cautiously slowed to a stop.

Ever fearful, she turned the radio off rolled the window down. There was no sound. The object hovered at about utility-pole height and spun toward and into a nearby clump of trees.

Satisfied that the craft had gone away, she continued driving the quarter-mile to her home. Her husband was working the overnight shift, so she immediately called a neighbor to report her strange experience.

The "thing" was nowhere to be seen when the

BERKS THE BIZARRE

neighbor arrived at her home to comfort her.

Soon after the neighbor departed, however, the object returned. It hovered near her yard for a brief time and departed.

At about 1 a.m., it returned. Throughout the following week, Mrs. Semmel saw the same object doing the same thing at about the same time. Again, she notified neighbors, but the elusive craft was seen only by the confused nurse.

It got to the point that Mrs. Semmel began to doubt her own sanity in this matter. She reported the incident to the State Police, who told her there was no aircraft in peril anywhere nearby.

A week after the initial sighting, neighbor Joyce Zettlemoyer was preparing to deliver the morning paper when she looked up to see an object which fit the description Mrs. Semmel gave.

Oval in shape and the size of a car or small aircraft, the craft hovered, its lights pulsating red and white.

"I'm glad she saw it too," Mrs. Semmel said at the time, "but I wish someone could explain it."

While the pros and cons of extraterrestrial travel were debated in Berks media and academia circles, more and more countians came forth with their stories.

Bonnie and Richard Jacoby of Hamburg said they saw an object hover near the borough on March 20. Red, white and blue lights blinked on it for about 20 minutes before it flew away.

More than a dozen Kutztown State College students also reported seeing something odd in the sky on the northeastern edge of that borough at about the same time.

Chief Earl Fox of the Fleetwood Police

141

BERKS THE BIZARRE

Department satisfied at least himself by claiming the flurry of reports could be traced to several spent fireworks cartridges he found along Crystal Cave Road during the time of the UFO reports.

Meanwhile, Dr. Ahmad Kiasat, an astronomy professor at Kutztown State, said flares on the surface of the sun at about the time of the sightings may have caused a so-called "Ray Aurora," which could have created the light show seen by the eyewitnesses.

Near the end of March, 1973, the Bunker Hill area of Western Berks was the next site of a sighting.

Clyde Donahower and his wife were asleep in their Robesonia-area home when, at about 1:30 in the morning, a screeching, rattling sound shook Mr. Donahower from his slumber.

He stumbled to a bedroom window, and was startled by what greeted his bleary eyes. He hastily awakened his wife.

"He couldn't believe what was seeing," Mrs. Donahower later related. "He wanted me to see it, too."

"It" was a lighted object which seemed to change its shape as it changed its color from a pale red to a pale green. Just before he was joined by his wife, Mr. Donahower claimed the UFO was aglow with a luminous brilliance.

As they watched, they were joined at the window by their eight-year old son. All remained silent, riveted to the field out back where one of the most incredible phenomena any human being could ever experience was playing out.

The family remained agape for nearly 20 minutes until, to their shock, they experienced what UFO

BERKS THE BIZARRE

researchers (and movie producers) call a "Close Encounter of the Third Kind."

"It was a black figure, like a stick figure, only thicker," Mr. Donahower told reporters. "It was moving in the center of the light. It was bending over and moving.

"It was scary. We were both frightened and fascinated."

That fear seemed to take over, and Mr. Donahower nervously dialed "O" to summon the police.

Heidelberg Township Police Chief Norman Brunner got the call, and arrived at the Donahower home by 2 a.m.

By the time he arrived, however, the object had simply faded from view. Chief Brunner and Mr. Donahower ventured into the plowed field where the latter had seen the strange object. There was no evidence of any landing, any beings, or any object.

Still, Chief Brunner did not discount their stories. He questioned the man, woman and child separately, and concluded, "I'm sure they saw something. Their stories were all consistent."

Clyde Donahower was somewhat tentative in his own assessment of the night's events.

"I was doubtful of what we were seeing. I'm still pretty skeptical. It was like a weird apparition."

That "apparition," or something very akin to it, seemed to dance across the Berks County sky throughout the night.

A multi-colored, luminous object was spotted by several residents of Cherokee Ranch, in Muhlenberg Township, and others in Mount Penn and Kutztown

143

BERKS THE BIZARRE

reported observing a similar thing.

In academic circles, professors at Kutztown State and Albright colleges were busy trying to explain the sightings away as meteorological, celestial or aviation realities.

But, Berks Countians continued to make headlines with their encounters of the first, second, third, and even *fourth* kind.

Curtis Lash was a strapping 25-year old when on March 29, 1973, he took a break from his carpet-laying job at a construction site on Rattlesnake Hill Road.

As he lit a cigarette, he was distracted by the lights of a silent, stationary object in the sky about a quarter-mile from where he was standing.

Its lights dimmed and brightened in no apparent pattern, and after it seemed to be joined by another similar craft, it seemed to vanish.

Lash, a former standout athlete at Schuylkill Valley High School, tried to tell his story to Ontelaunee Township police, but was too rattled by the events to fully explain at the time.

Police Sgt. Jack Rismiller said Lash was "really shaken up" when he talked to him. "There was no question that he was really scared," the sergeant said.

"I went home and tried to get some sleep," Lash said. "My eyes just wouldn't close. All I could see were those lights in the sky."

Lash affirmed that he did not believe in flying saucers, "but I know I saw something, and whatever it was was awful scary."

As the mini-hysteria continued, rural police officers made the news when they, too, reported UFOs in the sky over the Kutztown-Fleetwood areas.

BERKS THE BIZARRE

Kutztown patrolmen Paul B. Wary and Ronald Gardner observed a mysterious aircraft, and their police radio conversation regarding the observation alerted neighboring law enforcers.

Fleetwood P.D. Sgt. Richard L. Koller and Maidencreek P.D. Chief Alton Boyer all confirmed they caught glimpses of strange lights in the sky. Each refused to accept that the lights were those of an aircraft, star, satellite or weather balloon.

The next significant series of sightings came in 1976, when four persons in Robesonia witnessed three silvery, saucer-shaped objects fly in a neat formation about 300 feet off the ground, 100 yards from where they stood in amazement.

There was no noise, but strobe lights flashed from the crafts, each described as about 50 feet in diameter.

About the same time, six individuals watched what they called a cigar-shaped object hover over Strausstown.

One witness said that as airplanes flew high in the sky over it on several occasions, red sparks flickered from the mysterious entity.

Only scattered reports of unexplained "visitors" in the skies over Berks County were recorded in the 1980s.

In 1983, several glowing or flaming "fireballs" were seen by area residents, and some were reported to governmental authorities and/or private UFO investigative units. Nearly every one was explained and identified.

One of the most startling accounts of UFO and alien being incursion in Berks County was the revelation by a prominent African-American woman

145

that she had seen, and been touched by what she described as "a golden figure" in her city home.

Evelyn Morrison-Degler told a *Reading Eagle* reporter that her experiences with alien creatures dated to her childhood, when as a child on South 11th Street, she would have extra-sensory contacts with extra-terrestrials.

Through thoughts and physical contacts, Morrison-Degler claimed she continued to maintain relationships with the great beyond—be it spiritual or galactic.

In 1979, she said she was at Sixth and Oley Streets in Reading when she noticed three domed crafts circling over her head.

A figure she described as a gold in color and humanoid in shape, slowly dropped from one of the objects and took the stance of an archer several feet in front of her.

Dazed, the woman stood frozen as the being shot something into her right arm. "I became woozy, like I was drugged," she recalled.

"Then I slept," she continued, and I don't remember anything that happened until the next day."

That day, she said, she awakened to find herself standing by her car in the bright sunshine. A voice seemed to whisper, "Now you are immune."

Not sure what to make of all of it, Morrison-Degler got into her car. To further confuse her, the car started without her aid!

There are those who find accounts of Unidentified Flying Objects and the notion of E.T.s to be the stuff of the lunatic fringe.

And, there are those who have experienced a

BERKS THE BIZARRE

brush with the unknown who can neither discount or explain what they saw, heard or felt.

UFOs, and those who claim to have seen them, have been the butts of jokes since mankind was first introduced to "flying saucers" and "little green men".

In the midst of the raft of UFO sightings in metropolitan Reading in 1952, the city's mayor, James Bamford offered a whimsical explanation.

When asked his opinion of the "flying saucer" phenomenon, he told a Kiwanis Club gathering, "I think they're the tops blown by people who have appeared in city hall of the past seven months!"

BB

BERKS THE BIZARRE
UNEASY IN OLEY

It is hard to imagine the quiet, quaint village of Oley as ever having its own brothel.

But, that's just what some folks in town say a tiny portion of an old home in the heart of town used to be.

And, the present residents of the handsome, hundred year-old home say the old place may be haunted.

The building's alleged illicit heritage may have nothing whatsoever to do with the "things that go bump in the night" these days, but the tenants are a tad uneasy from time to time when the spooks seem to be at their spunkiest.

From the deep sills in a drafty but pleasant parlor, one may look out to the steady flow of traffic on Main Street. Intricate stenciling caps walls otherwise devoid of adornment.

The "main" house, once believed to have been a doctor's office, is joined to what was a neighboring structure with a "shed". It is within the walls of that makeshift connector where the red light of local legend was once lit.

While none were available to discuss it, many former owners and tenants reportedly had untoward encounters in the place.

The current tenant, whom we shall call Kathy, recalled one former owner's childhood experience.

"Her parents' bed had to be against a certain wall," she said. "If the parents moved that bed against a different wall, they would be approached by the ghost of a man. The woman I talked to told me that as a child, if she would sit on her parents' bed, she would see that figure."

The tiny bedroom in question is actually quite uncompromising in how any bed could be placed.

Kathy has never seen the ghostly figure in the room, maybe because her bed is against the prescribed wall.

She does say a light in the room has a habit of turning itself on from time to time, and her daughter claims a closet door jiggles–but the source of their uneasiness is not in the bedroom, or the old brothel.

It's in a place where many people fear to tread–the attic.

"It's an uneasy feeling," Kathy said. "There was one time it really scared us. My daughter and I were upstairs in our beds. I had just turned the lights off and all of a sudden I started hearing this scratching against the door."

Her first inclination was to blame it on a cat, or a wayward squirrel. She said it was too loud, too strong, to be either. "It was like two hands going real strong," she recalled. "I turned the light on. I was scared."

The scratching went on for about 15 minutes, and each grinding stroke seemed to run the full length of the attic door.

That same door has, on occasion, opened by itself. And, the family dog seems to be acutely aware of an unseen presence, sometimes staring wide-eyed up the staircase to the attic.

Even Kathy's friend, Bill, who remains skeptical, has admitted to hearing mysterious footfalls on the stairs.

Kathy has reluctantly discussed her plight with neighbors, and they have reluctantly told her that they

BERKS THE BIZARRE

have seen a ghostly figure moving past upstairs windows both when Kathy was and was not home.

Who it is, what it is, are real concerns for Kathy. Nothing horrifying has yet taken place in the house, but there have been episodes strong enough to send her 9-year old scurrying into her mom's bed for security.

Kathy remains hopeful that it all can be explained away somehow, sometime.

"I would be very satisfied in knowing there was absolutely nothing in this house," she said nervously. "That would not bother me one bit.

"But, when you're told some guy's ghost lives (so to speak) in your attic, it's a little upsetting!"

BB

BERKS THE BIZARRE
"WE MISS HIM SO MUCH..."

The setting was hardly one you'd expect on a hunt for ghostly activity.

We sat on the pleasant patio of a typical suburban home in Temple. Birds chirped gaily in the trees, an occasional car passed by, and the interviewees nodded and greeted neighbors who walked along the sidewalk.

The woman whose story would soon unfold has had several psychic and supernatural experiences over her lifetime, but was generally indistinguishable from the other mothers and wives who lived in the houses around hers.

We sipped iced tea on that summer afternoon, and after the usual small talk wound down, the discussion grew ghostly.

It centered on a man she called Chet. He was a close friend of the woman's mother, a strapping man who spent many hours and days in her house. He shared in the family's joys and challenges, and became a second father to the young woman.

It was several years ago, and the woman was preparing for her coming marriage. It was supposed to be the happiest time of her life.

Then came the news. Chet was on a fishing trip in the northern woods. There was a terrible accident, and her dear Chet was killed.

The mother was devastated. Daughter, too, felt the pain of the loss. Still, the woman went through with the marriage plans, and mother and daughter tried their best to cope with the loss of Chet.

"Then," the woman said, "one evening close to the time to the wedding, I was sitting at a window. I

151

saw a white form, from shoulders up, go past the window, looking down at the ground.

"That was that. It was gone. I never feel uneasy about it. I almost wish I could have communicated with it. But, maybe I'm better off not knowing."

The woman stared into the trees for a moment, gathered her senses, and continued.

"Another time, I was in the living room looking out toward the kitchen and I just had a feeling. I happened to look up and standing in the doorway, between the kitchen and the living room, was a full form, about six feet tall.

"Once again, there was no uneasiness about it. I wasn't uncomfortable. It was almost a comforting feeling. I think I knew then who it was."

It was, she truly believes to this day, Chet.

After the wedding, she confided her tales to her new husband. He listened, but scoffed at the notion that a ghost could be haunting his wife.

"Sometime after I was married," she continued, "I was in the living room again and I looked out and saw a white cloud floating over the saloon doors into the next room."

As the woman told her stories, her young son sat by her side, fully supportive of his mother.

She added that her mother has a friend who professes to have psychic powers. She had independently confirmed that the spirit of a man does indeed reside in the family's home.

The woman's voice grew shaky, her eyes moistened, and she concluded her simple but poignant story.

She recounted the times the apparition made itself

BERKS THE BIZARRE

known. She sketched details of the days before her wedding, her married life, and the subsequent divorce.

"I think it really was Chet out there, somewhere. He just wanted to let me know he was there whenever I needed him, that's all."

A tear coursed its way down her cheek as she said, through words now broken by emotion, "We miss him so much..."

Maybe, just maybe, there's no reason to miss him at all. Maybe, just maybe, old Chet never really left.

BB

BERKS THE BIZARRE
CENTER-CITY SPOOKS

Although they are obscured by tall buildings, busy streets and high church steeples, there is a handful of graveyards in downtown Reading, and in one of them may still be seen the ghost of a lovely, young woman and–perhaps–a headless man with a drawn sword, mounted on a milk white horse.

The tale persisted in the mid-19th century that when night enveloped the town of Reading in darkness, the ghosts of the Trinity Lutheran Church graveyard would come out to haunt.

Hundreds of people swore they actually saw the ghosts, and skittish citizens refused to pass by the tiny cemetery after dark, fearing they'd come across the mysterious "lady in white".

Not much was known about the strange denizen of the dark, but witnesses said her hazy image could often be spotted seated silently and motionlessly on a tombstone just inside the wall of the Trinity Lutheran church yard.

Not seen as often was the shadowy form of what was described as a headless man, seemingly clad in full body armor.

One arm was raised and a sword flailed from his fist. He was atop a sturdy, white stallion.

Those who came across this ominous apparition said it was not clearly defined, and often wavered in form. What they described, though, is what they saw.

Just down the street, at the old Court House–then located in what is now the middle of the Fifth and Penn Streets intersection–another ghost was blamed for peculiarities in the clock tower.

BERKS THE BIZARRE

"Ferhext," the building's janitor said. Ghosts or hobgoblins got into the mechanism, he figured.

The clock bell was rigged so it would not sound at night, but on several occasions, it would strike and send a disturbing knell through the slumbering neighborhood.

Other times, when the bell was supposed to peal, it did not.

"Ferhext," exclaimed the janitor.

More than a few times, the caretaker had to climb into the clock tower–two, three, four times a night. Each time, nothing seemed to be mechanically wrong.

But, was it a ghost? Was the clock tower of the Court House indeed "ferhext?"

What's more, was there truly the ghost of a "lady in white" who shared the Trinity Lutheran Church graveyard with the headless horseman?

Sadly, probably not.

An article in the Berks and Schuylkill Journal newspaper in April, 1873, exploded the ghost stories as the work of pranksters who toyed with the superstitions of the townsfolk.

There really was a long-standing rumor that a ghost did (and still does) inhabit the Trinity Lutheran graveyard.

Knowing this, and hoping to perpetuate the story and petrify the citizenry, a young woman decided to designate the graveyard as the site of a rendezvous between her and a suitor who had fallen out of favor with her parents and was not allowed in or even near her home.

She always dressed in a long, white dress, and sat motionlessly on a tombstone until her male friend

BERKS THE BIZARRE

would pass by. At that cue, she would skulk into the night and meet him around the corner.

As for the headless horseman, it was generally dismissed as nothing more than the shadows thrown by the branches of an apple tree across the street.

The Court House "hex" was eventually dismissed as the work of pranksters who rigged up a cord from the clapper of the bell to a second floor window in the old State House. From their lair, they would pull the cord, sound the bell, and send the caretaker (and, no doubt, nearby slumberers) into conniptions.

Two other sites were the settings for 19th century ghost stories, and neither of their ethereal inhabitants was ever explained away so easily.

It could well be, then, that a ghost still does haunt the Penn Street Bridge, and another wanders the city side of Neversink Mountain.

Not much is known about the Neversink ghost, but there is at least the framework of the origins of the spook on the span.

It was fairly well documented that at least one person chose the old covered bridge across the Schuylkill as a suitable suicide spot.

One of the men found hanged inside the old bridge, was said to have never really left the place.

His ghost was seen ambling across the covered bridge, its iron successor, and, some say, the present structure.

BB

BERKS THE BIZARRE
LADY IN WHITE

While there is no one place in Berks County which could be considered the vortex of supernatural activity, two diverse geographical regions seem to hold within them very powerful paranormal energies.

The Oley Valley and Hawk Mountain are unquestionably the most "haunted" areas of the county. On the northwestern ridge of the Oley Valley is Pricetown, and around that crossroads village are many legends and tales of ghostly encounters.

The exact location has been lost in time, but somewhere along the Pricetown Road between Breezy Corners and Pricetown the sad spirit of a lady in white has been sighted by several witnesses over the last few decades.

One of those who reported such a sighting was a local police officer who told his comrades he was in his personal car, off-duty, when he encountered the mysterious woman in white.

More accurately, it was a woman in gray, and according to the officer, only the rough shape of the ghostly form led him to believe it was female.

"I was coming home from Reading," he said. "I hadn't been drinking or anything. I was just past Breezy Corners when on my right, walking with its back to me, was a woman or something. It looked like a woman with fairly long hair and an ankle-length dress.

"It was just about dusk, and still very light. It had been a very nice day. This individual, though, seemed to be very gray in color, from top to bottom.

"I know it sounds unbelievable, but it seemed to

glow or emit some dim light of its own. I saw it very clearly, and since it was about 50 yards ahead of me when I first saw it, I kept it in my sights for quite some time.

"It moved very slowly, and as I remember, it seemed to glide along smoothly. I don't mind saying I was a little confused and a little put off by it.

"As I approached her, or it, or whatever, I slowed down. I kept my attention on my driving and tried to look at the figure as long as I could out of the corner of my eye.

"Then, I was about 20 feet away from it and driving very slowly. There were no cars coming, or anywhere in sight, so I slowed to a crawl.

"Now, I *know* the figure was there all along, but in the second or so it took for me to check any nearby traffic, it was gone."

The officer, who requested anonymity in exchange for his story, said he was a bit shaken by the experience.

"As long as I live," he said, "I will remember exactly what happened that day. I don't tell too many people about it because they listen, but I can always detect that they don't believe."

There are other tales which are logged in the ledger of the lore of Ruscombmanor Township.

One dates to the early 1900s, and is centered at the intersection of Pricetown Road and Route 662.

In the January 1, 1954, edition of *The Pennsylvania Dutchman* magazine, an anonymous author related ghost stories told to him by his father.

"I remember that pop used to talk about this one particular ghost, but would never tell me all about it.

BERKS THE BIZARRE

"Later on I did find out what it was all about. There is a big old chestnut tree standing up near the corner at Pricetown. And years ago, when the roads were built by pick and shovel there used to be spooks up there.

"People used to have to pass this big tree. It had immense big roots, and at night when they used to pass it they would see a dog without a head or a horse without a head and even some of the people said they saw a *man* without a head along this old road at night.

"It would scare the people out of their wits and that was why it spooked the place.

"This happened until one day the people came to fix the road and they dug along the road. When they got to the chestnut tree they dug and as they hit the roots some bones rolled out.

"The men ran all scared and excited because they didn't know if the bones were of a dog or a human.

"The funny thing was that after they dug, there were no more ghosts!"

In the same account, the writer told of the phantom horse whose ghost gallops in the night in a field along the Pricetown Road.

On quiet nights when there is little moonlight, the faint sound of hoof beats can be heard in the distance.

To those who are brave enough to linger, the muffled clippety-clop grows louder and from the direction they are heard a glow begins to form.

At once, the image of a white horse forms.

It approaches at full gallop, but it seems to be just above ground level.

Closer it speeds toward you. And then, as you cower in fear and confusion, the steed rises and soars

BERKS THE BIZARRE

into the night sky and vanishes!

The anonymous author of a 1954 article on ghost in *The Pennsylvania Dutchman* magazine did not pinpoint when or where this phenomenon took place, but said his uncle told him it happened somewhere along the Pricetown Road, and swore it was true.

The writer did attribute some tales to folks who allowed their names to be used.

Elaborating on legends in and around Ruscombmanor Township, one Nathan Berky recalled an old lime kiln between Pricetown and Oley from which a ghost would occasionally peek out. And, Berky said, the intersection of Pricetown Road and Skyline Drive was always said to be haunted by one or more spirits.

Berky also had many stories from deeper in the Oley Valley. "I remember how my wife's parents and grandpop used to talk about seeing things," Berky said. "When they used to live down in Oley, they would at certain times on some nights see a man with a long white beard that looked out of the second story window at the people. And yet, there was never nobody there."

Arlene Smith, whom the writer identified as a "third cousin" also provided an interesting interpretation of a strange but surprisingly common phenomenon some people call "spirit lights".

Throughout the lore of Berks County farm families are recurring reports of lights which appear mysteriously in fields. They could glow brightly as distinct points of brilliance or be indistinct balls of phosphorescence.

They could hover as if suspended over the ground

or bob and weave wildly.

Erde Lichte, the old-timers called them—Earth Lights.

Spirit lights, earth lights—whatever they are called— they are quite disconcerting to those who encounter them.

Arlene Smith had some stories about, and some possible explanations for the farm yard phenomena.

In the words of the nameless author, "She would tell us of how when they used to live in Oley on the big farm, on certain nights they would see these lights moving around in the barnyard.

"She said that the closer you got to them the further away they would move. They were never stationary and when you stood still they seemed to move towards you.

"They were like a big ball of light, something like an electric light but with a bluish-yellow tinge. She said you could see them any time of the year, especially in the spring.

"Others say they can only be seen on damp nights, or on foggy nights or in February.

"They are ghostly in action and appearance. From all the sources of these lights we must assume that they are actually present and not a figmentation of the imagination. Too many people swear they have seen them at one time or another.

"As for an explanation as to how they are present I can offer none. The lights could be present because of a leak in the oil line or because of dead bodies buried beneath the earth at these particular places or because of the reflection of the moon upon dew or some other object—or maybe a bit of imagination is accountable.

BERKS THE BIZARRE

"Whatever the case may be, they are a physical being and must be explained or condemned."

Closing this chapter on the book of the strange in Ruscombmanor Township, we relate a story which is typical of those told in the pre-TV era, when the mind was teased and terrified not by electronic emissions but by electrified imaginations.

Gideon Fries lived near the old Weber's Hotel, and as a teenager he knew of the ghost which could be heard but not seen along a fence near a farm on the road between Pricetown and Oley.

One night, Gideon decided he would stalk the spirit and try to catch a glimpse of the ghost which was said to wander past unsuspecting folks and give off the eerie sound of chains rattling and dragging.

Sure enough, he dared to venture to the appointed spot and heard the chains. Try as he might have to be brave, he instead ran in utter fear as the sound grew closer.

The next morning, he told his mother of his encounter. Her sense of adventure was piqued, and she offered to accompany her son to the area and uncover this chain-rattling ghost.

Together, they hiked to the fence and to where Gideon had his experience the night before.

It was not in the dark of night, but the light of day. Still, to mother and son's amazement, the faint jangle of chains rose as if from nowhere. As they walked on, the clamor intensified.

They approached a barn. It was from there that the rattling chatter came.

Hand in hand, Gideon and his mother tiptoed toward the barn. With wide eyes, they peered toward the source of the chain-dragging ghost.

Simultaneously, their eyes widened, their necks stiffened, and they saw the "ghost" which hitherto could only be heard.

Huddled in the muddy barn yard was a mother pig with several piglets feeding on her.

Chortling, sucking, smacking sounds bounced off the barn wall.

Under the morning sun, the sound was clearly identifiable for what it was.

On a moonless night, alone on a dark back road, it would be easy to imagine the sharp grunting and snorting noises to be anything else–including that of a chain-dragging ghost.

BB

BERKS THE BIZARRE
THE SOLDIER'S GHOST
AT MENSCH MILL

The folks at the Pennsylvania Southeast Conference of the United Church of Christ knew what they were doing when they converted the 1810-era Mensch Mill property into a church-operated retreat center in 1928.

They inherited one of the prettiest spots in Berks County. The old Mensch house holds a conference room, kitchen and dining room, and bedroom units which will accommodate up to 20 guests.

At the restored mill across the way are four more dorm-style rooms, and eight cabins can accommodate even more visitors.

Other meeting and recreation rooms are located in a barn and outbuildings on the rocky slope which leads from the tranquil Vesper Hill to a pond.

Around the pond is a nature trail from which paddle boats, fishing and other aquatic diversions may be viewed.

The West Branch of the Perkiomen Creek babbles as a waterfall into the pond, and beyond a small dam are giant boulders which face the mill stream and the giant, old mill building.

The Mensch Mill Retreat Center's beauty is not to be outdone by its historical importance.

A monument erected in 1915 by the Historical Society of Berks County stands precariously near the entrance to the nature trail and waterfall.

Molded in the shape of a classic ironmaking-era stove, the memorial honors the Hereford Furnace, which was located nearby.

It was there, between 1734 and 1788, that under ironmaster Thomas Mabury, the first cook stove made in America was produced.

Incredibly, that stove is still secreted inside one of the retreat buildings. A simple plaque marks its significance.

The camp, just around a country road corner from Huff's Church in the panhandle of Hereford Township, is indeed a pleasant blend of beauty and history.

To put a little spice in the serenity and some shadows beyond the camp fire, is also a ghost story.

The tale was told in the 1940s by Dr. William Hartman, who had been a counselor at Camp Mensch Mill in the early 1930s.

Young Bill Hartman and his fellow counselors were between sessions and spending a quiet weekend waiting for the next campers to arrive.

With most of the transitional labors completed, Bill and a comrade decided to seek out a building near the camp which was supposedly haunted.

Everybody in the area knew the place as the old haunted house. Its exact location has been forgotten over ensuing decades.

They said, though, that the old place was haunted by the ghost of a Hessian soldier who had escaped from his unit during the Revolutionary War and had sought refuge in the remote home.

Instead of aid and comfort, the poor soldier met his death at the hands of an unknown killer.

The story was told that the German mercenary was brutally murdered in the cellar of what was even then an old house. His slayer fled and was never

BERKS THE BIZARRE

brought to justice.

After the body of the poor Hessian was discovered and buried in an unmarked grave, folks in the rugged glen which cuts between two rocky rises with the ominous names of Devil Head and Blackhead Hill immediately began to report unusual and terrifying sights and sounds in the ancient place.

The soldier's ghost was spotted wandering through the forest, and in the old farm house.

Bill Hartman and his camp cohort wandered just off the camp grounds to the haunted house. If they were brave enough, they figured they would spend that Saturday night inside the abandoned building.

As the sun set over Devil Head, they reached their gloomy destination. Armed with a sense of adventure and flashlights, they found an open door and ventured inside.

The floorboards on the main floor creaked beneath their weight. The delicate scratching of birds' claws on the roof were magnified by the stark silence. A squirrel—or could it have been a rat—scurried from its hiding place.

The strapping young men were determined to ferret out the ghost and return to the camp with their tales of bravado.

There was an overpowering musty smell about the place, and always the sense of wide-eyed anticipation that behind the next wall or beyond the next door, the ghost of the murdered man may appear.

The intrepid pair carefully ascended a rickety staircase to the second floor and explored each room.

No ghost was found.

But it was the cellar, the old stories maintained, in

BERKS THE BIZARRE

which the soldier was slain. If there really was a resident wraith, would it not most likely dwell in the darkness between the foundation walls?

Bill's buddy decided to head outside for a smoke, leaving the future physician alone in the eerie house.

Biding his time on the first floor until his friend returned, Bill came across a trap door which led to the basement.

His curiosity got the best of him, and alone he lowered himself into the subterranean space.

Pitch black and damp, the cellar was a forbidding room, even to the young and daring man.

As soon as his soles planted themselves onto the dirt floor of the cellar, Bill had the feeling other souls may be looking over his shoulder, lurking in the cobwebbed corners.

Then, he saw it.

In one of the corners, a dim glow cut through the darkness. Bill's attention was riveted to whatever it could have been.

The glow grew brighter and split in two. As he stood frozen in fear, Bill watched as what he could only describe as two luminous eyes stared back at him.

Brighter and brighter they became until they seemed to lunge at the terror-stricken camp counselor.

In a flash, it was all over.

All Bill could recall later was waking up outside the house, still trembling from the encounter.

The young men gathered their flashlights, and their senses, and hastened to the safety of the camp.

Nights before the campfire there would never be the same again!

BB

BERKS THE BIZARRE
THE BIZARRE OLD DAYS

At one time or another in everyone's life, they catch themselves waxing fondly about "the good old days".

In this chapter, we stray a bit from the other-world of ghosts and legends and dig between the lines of Berks County's popular history.

The following anecdotes will suffice to suggest that while there indeed may have been "good old days", even those days were peppered with the bizarre.

For those who support the proposition that there's nothing new under the sun, consider this snippet from the November 20, 1895, *Reading Eagle*.

"On most any pleasant day you can find a lot of boys, ranging in age from 8 to 18 years, playing cards along the main Philadelphia and Reading railroad tracks between the Bingaman Street Bridge and the furnace plug."

Such was the statement of a veteran railroader whose declaration made the front page of the paper that day.

The revelation that these minors were gathered on the wrong side of the hooky track shocked the inquiring reporter.

When the scribe asked the railroader what kind of games they would play, he responded, "Poker. And, for money!"

The railroad man claimed the boys would pick coal from the railroad bed–"or steal it"–and sell it to gather their poker stakes.

The informant further revealed, "Several times the

BERKS THE BIZARRE

games were so exciting that the youngsters fought until some had bloody noses.

"The authorities should take hold of this matter and break up the practice," he lamented. "These boys should be at school, and perhaps their parents think they are."

BB

As you adjust the air conditioning on your car when you drive through a sweltering downtown Reading in the summer, consider the plight of the poor horses which pulled wagons through town around the turn of the century.

In July, 1901, news broke of a novel practice which was sweeping through the equine world as the days grew warmer.

"To prevent heat prostration, a straw bonnet is the latest novelty for horses in Reading," reported an *Eagle* writer.

Citing its beneficial effect in "keeping the brain center cool," the horse hat was endorsed by the Society for the Prevention of Cruelty to Animals and was widely accepted by riders and owners of horses throughout the city.

The newspaper article included a pair of illustrations, "How the hats are worn," with one hand-drawn picture featuring a rather silly-looking ash-cart horse sporting his owner's derby.

The custom-made straw horse hats were conical with two slits in the brim through which the steed's ears were fitted.

Prospective horse hat fitters were advised to leave a "space for the breeze to play" and not place the hat tightly on the animal's head.

169

BERKS THE BIZARRE

Not only were the hats beneficial to the horse's health, the newspaper reporter added they "lend a chic air" to any beast who wears one.

§§

The old-fashioned "shoe-shine boy" or "bootblack" is a precious and somewhat anachronistic commodity these days.

Nearly a century ago, however, in the days before suede and cloth footwear, bootblacks were so common in Reading that they considered forming a union which would work for the common good of all.

The news to the man on the street was that any such move by the nearly three dozen bootblacks who had gathered on North Sixth Street might result in a higher price for a shine.

The men who met considered themselves "professionals", and were angered by the incursion of what they called "tramp" bootblacks who drove the prices—and the quality—of the "pro" jobs down.

E. Raymond Reese, the chief organizer, pointed out that bootblacks in other cities such as Lancaster had already banded together to protect their product and themselves.

"Professor Frank" Whitfield, one of the best-known bootblacks in the city, suggested that no one could learn the fine art of shoe shining in less than a year, and an apprentice system might help advance the cause of the serious shiners.

It was estimated that if the move would take hold, as many as 50 Reading bootblacks could become members of the "union".

As for the price hike, it was generally believed that a full doubling of the cost of a shine from the prevailing

170

BERKS THE BIZARRE

nickel to a dime would not strap the customers. "I have only six five-cent customers," one bootblack said, "and the others voluntarily pay ten cents. I think that we should be given a raise. Every trade is getting higher wages and shorter hours, and we ought to get something!"

ßß

February, 1905: The county treasurer reported there were $34,175.23 in the county's general fund. The "sleighing was excellent" on the county's snow-covered roads. And, members of the Independent Gun Club of Reading dined on the victims of their recent live pigeon shoot at the Three-Mile House.

It was not a good day for Lucas Niklos of the 200 block of Cedar Street, Reading.

A laborer at a city factory, Niklos had emigrated from Hungary three years before. Described as a good worker and a worthy husband, the 36-year old had spent what his wife, Frances, described as a restless night.

It was four in the morning when Frances shook Niklos and reminded him he had to get up for work. He mumbled, tossed, and turned over. Satisfied that he was awake and aware, Frances walked to an adjoining room. Within minutes she heard her husband holler from the other room, "I'll never go to work again!"

In another few seconds, she heard the sound of a single gun shot. A bullet in his right temple ensured that his deathbed declaration would be a self-fulfilling prophecy.

Lucas Niklos would not report to work that morning, or any other morning, ever.

ßß

171

BERKS THE BIZARRE

AUF WIEDERSEHEN, JANE

Ghostly tales abound within the comfortable confines of the Genesius Theater on North Tenth Street in Reading.

It seems that every initiate to the company of players is introduced at some point in their apprenticeship to the unexplained sounds and sensations which lurk somewhere in the darkened corners and niches of the building.

Generations of actors and actresses, directors and artists, musicians and patrons at Genesius have reported untoward and unexpected encounters, and in this chapter we dig deep into our files for an interview conducted several years ago with a man who was once quite active in Genesius productions.

Larry Fecho has moved on to other places and projects, but at the time of our talk, he was plunged head-first into Genesius.

Fecho, who later managed operations at the (haunted) Fulton Opera House in Lancaster, didn't hesitate to pin much of the supernatural sources at Genesius to the building itself and to one dynamic and legendary person.

"At community theaters such as Genesius," Fecho said, "there is a rare kind of intimacy between the cast and the audience. That intimacy lends itself to strange and wondrous emotions, individuals and incidents."

One such wondrous individuals was Jane Simmon Miller.

In her ascent through local theatrical ranks, Jane was often considered a theatrical rebel—a daring and innovative performer, producer and director.

172

BERKS THE BIZARRE

"I never thought of her as being real," Fecho said. He was barely in his teens when he first met Jane Miller. "There was always something sort of magical about her. People either really loved her or hated her. There was no in between.

"She did a lot with Reading Community Players before she started Genesius. She told some incredible stories from Community. We'd sit there at Genesius and it'd be dark and dank and she'd tell these stories.

"It was during their show 'Tom Jones.' A lady with a lead part in the cast had cancer and was dying. Opening night, the woman died. Jane had to go on that night.

"For about a year or two, they would hear noises up there. Jane would be in the theater alone and she'd spend a lot of time making costumes. She'd always hear people talking–a lone male voice, groups, all kinds of sounds. They were eerie stories."

Described by Fecho as a true "spirit of the theater", it may well be that Jane Miller is indeed *the* spirit of Genesius Theater!

"Death never bothered Jane," he continued. "If there's one thing in this world I would like to have, it would be that kind of flamboyant attitude Jane had."

"She had been very ill, but was very determined to make Genesius a viable theater in town."

"At Genesius then, most of us were just kids. The other theaters didn't like us, but we struggled."

Jane was quite realistic about her own mortality. "She told us that if they played funeral music on an organ at her viewing, she'd come back and haunt us. We all listened closely to her desires.

"She died on the closing night of Cabaret at

BERKS THE BIZARRE

Genesius. The last words in the show are "...auf wiedersehen, good night.

"The performer who said those words was Brian Gibson, who was very close to Jane.

"At the closing night cast party, someone had to tell everyone that she had died. It was odd. There were many tears, but there were also those who, under their breaths, muttered 'Ding, Dong, the Witch is Dead'. Such was Jane's personality."

Fecho recalled hearing from one of Jane's relatives in Robeson Township who told him that the night of her death, a presence appeared in their home and assured them gently that all was well and death had come quietly.

That relative was Karen Lee P. Miller, now Karen Sterner, and a resident of Largo, Florida.

Karen said the incident involved her then-four year old son Morgan, Jane's grandson.

"Morgan was put to bed," Ms. Sterner wrote in a letter to this author, "and woke up crying that someone was walking around in his bedroom."

At that particular time, Karen noted, her son had no knowledge that his grandmother had passed away.

"A few days later, my mother's sister Barbara came from out of town to attend the funeral," Karen continued. "Barbara's bedroom was directly above ours and during the night my husband, Chris, and I heard someone walking around in that room.

"The next morning we asked Barbara about the footsteps and she said she also heard them but thought it was 'just my sister Jane coming back to say goodbye.'

"We had not relayed the previous incident of the

174

footsteps in Morgan's room to her because at the time it seemed like a child's wakeful dream."

Those inexplicable incidents aside, the realities of Jane Miller's funeral warrant recollection.

"She was buried in a gold lame dress, which was her favorite," Fecho said.

"We had roses, and thousands of people came to the funeral parlor in Mt. Penn. We had an ad in the paper for the 'Final Curtain Call' for Jane Simmon Miller. Her viewing was under the proscenium arch of the funeral parlor.

"They played a tape of the music from shows she had done, and at the actual service, they sang her favorite song, 'This My Friend is Only the Beginning,' from *The Roar of the Greasepaint, the Smell of the Crowd.* Then, they closed the curtain."

Fecho remembered the day of the burial as a bright, sunny one.

"The only thing was, that Jane hated sunshine. She liked misty kind of days.

"We had a long procession to Alsace Lutheran Cemetery. As we pulled into the graveyard, it started to rain, as if on cue.

"And honestly, as we left the cemetery after the service, the rain stopped, the sun came back out–again, as if on cue."

Was this all the overture for a drama which continues to play out on and off the Genesius stage?

"When we took the place over," Fecho said of the genesis of Genesius, "it was the Northeast Republican Club. We found all kinds of strange things in the building.

"The room where they have their costumes

BERKS THE BIZARRE

now—where Jane hung out all the time—was where they used to have their secret political meetings back in the old days."

That traditional "smoke-filled room" where GOP bosses once planned and plotted party fortunes is now filled with another kind of ethereal power.

A young woman Larry Fecho had dated once toiled in what became the costume room and was introduced to the ghostly presence.

"Jane always wore short heels, and my friend heard the distinct sound of a woman walking across the floor of the dark room in heels.

"There's this little slit through which you can look into or out of the room, and she looked through it, only to see a pair of eyes looking back of her. She ran like crazy, because it scared the hell out of her."

Fecho said he felt the ghost availed itself to newcomers at the theater, and felt it was definitely that of Jane Simmon Miller.

He also affirmed that if, indeed, the spirit was that of Jane, those who encountered it would have nothing to fear.

"I remember one time when Melissa Gallagher came off for a dress change during one of the shows, she started to fall off a platform. She swore to God that these two hand grabbed her and pushed her back up. She felt it was Jane."

Many other unexplained sounds, sights, and feelings have manifested before those who have passed—and continue to pass—through the labyrinth of rooms of Genesius Theater.

Most folks, like Larry Fecho, believe it is the irrepressible energy of Jane Simmon Miller which

BERKS THE BIZARRE

remains locked within the walls she helped transform from a hall of political intrigue to a respected community theater.

"With Jane, you just knew that she wouldn't pass away into oblivion. You sort of knew she'd always be around, somewhere, in some way.

Perhaps the woman once described as the "spirit of Reading theater" is indeed the spirit of one of those theaters.

BB

BERKS THE BIZARRE
KEEPING THE SECRET

"All I know is that I never want to see anything like that again."

The words broke nervously from the lips of a 28-year old Boyertown-area professional man who opted to not permit his name to be revealed.

Just what did this gentleman experience that shook him to the roots of his sensibilities?

"Right from the start, I must tell you that the idea of ghosts and life after death and all that has never been a priority in my mind. Of course, I saw some movies with those themes, but mostly because of the actors or actresses, not because I was particularly interested in the subject matter.

"Anyway, I just want you to know that I was not predisposed toward ghosts and goblins. Not at all. But after what happened, I've changed my opinion of it all."

The man–we shall call him Rick–said a weird chain of events started when he visited the home of a friend in the rolling countryside between Boyertown and Pine Forge.

"He and his wife lived in a lovely old farmhouse," Rick said. "They paid very little for it because it needed a lot of work.

"They had been there about two months and had done a lot of work to that point. All the windows were replaced and they put on a new roof.

"I got to their place just after dark and we were going to watch a video together. My wife was away on a trip, and they kidded that they would 'babysit' me for a night.

BERKS THE BIZARRE

"We had a pizza, and I asked them to show me around the house before we settled in for the movie. We went upstairs, to the master bedroom they were working on.

"My first inkling that something was up was on the second set of stairs which led to the upstairs hall. I was lagging a few steps behind them when I absolutely, positively felt a pressure–it's hard to describe–some sort of invisible force–rub against my shoulder.

"It wasn't a temperature change, or a breeze, or anything. It was as if something was really there. It wasn't solid, it was gaseous, I guess. That's what I mean, it's hard to describe.

"Anyway, it was just a second's worth of distraction, and I tried to ignore it. Then, I reached the top of the steps when my eyes were somehow diverted by something in the doorway of one of the bedrooms.

"Again, it happened in a flash. But I know, I absolutely know, that there was something in the doorway.

"We got together at the door to the master bedroom, and I didn't let on as to what I had felt and seen on the way. So, we just stood around and they told me about the work they had done and the work they had planned. I must admit, though, that I was more than a little on edge.

"Actually, I only caught about half of what they were saying. My mind kept wandering back to that sensation on the steps and that vision in the doorway.

"We walked down the hallway toward the door at which I saw that...that form. That's when everything got a little scary."

179

BERKS THE BIZARRE

Even over the telephone line, Rick was audibly shaken by the episode. He composed himself, heaved a deep sigh, and continued his story.

"My buddy kidded around when we got to that particular door," he continued. "He was a little like me, I guess. He pointed into that room and sort of chuckled that 'that room is our *haunted* room!' He brushed over it quickly, saying that a past resident had killed himself in the room, and some folks who had lived in the house swear they could see his ghostly form in the room.

"Well, that set me back a little. I didn't want to belabor the topic, but I had to know more. Sheepishly, I asked if he knew anything else about that. He said he didn't.

"I didn't want to let the matter drop, but I felt it was best for the time being to do so. We went through the rest of the house, and settled down to the movie.

"Well, nature called to me an hour or so later, and I wandered back upstairs to the bathroom. Remembering what I felt before, I climbed the steps hoping to–and, I guess, hoping not to–feel something again. Simply stated, I felt nothing.

"But sure enough, as I approached the second floor, I clearly saw, standing in that same doorway, a figure. This time, I could definitely make out the shape of a human being. There was no doubt. As crazy as it sounds, I saw a human form standing in that doorway.

"Of course, it frightened me a bit. I stared at it, and could feel my heart racing. It was probably only about five or six seconds, but it was long enough for me to realize that whatever I was looking at was, how can I say it, not quite solid. There were no features like eyes or a mouth or anything. I can't recall any clothing or colors. It was, well, just *there.*"

Rick chose not to say a word to his hosts. He kept his secret and decided to pursue another course of action.

"I just couldn't let it go. I did a little investigative work and tried to find out who died there, how and when he died, and who may have reported seeing the ghost.

"I didn't have to go far. As it turned out, I knew one of the neighbors who was around when the man killed himself in the farmhouse. He gave me all the details I needed.

"It turned out that the man took an overdose of sleeping pills, or some kind of drugs, in that upstairs bedroom. He died a quiet death, but his suicide note was very revealing.

"The neighbor understood that in the note, the man admitted that he had been unfaithful to his wife, had financial troubles, and was in trouble with the law. He had all kinds of stuff going on.

"The first person the neighbor knew who had any kind of sighting of the man's ghost was the victim's brother. He had come in to help clean out the house after the suicide.

"Now, you must understand that the neighbor I was talking to had no idea what I experienced that night when I was visiting. That's why I kind of shuddered when he told me the rest of the story.

"He said the man's brother had come into the house and was making his way up the stairs when he felt something brush past him halfway up. And, when he got to the top, he saw the form of his brother standing in the doorway of the room in which he killed himself.

"A couple days later, he went back to the house to do more work, and the same thing happened again.

"He said the form never spoke, there were no distinguishable features, and it faded away in a few seconds.

"It was all just, too uncanny, to say the least."

Rick said he would probably never tell his story to his friends. He didn't want to "spook" them or let them know that he had seen what he can only describe today as a ghost.

Of course, if his friends are reading this now, and they can put two and two together, they now know Rick's secret.

BB

BERKS THE BIZARRE
THE "DOCTOR'S" ORDERS

In the late 19th century, it was not unusual for a story about hexes, witchcraft and ghosts to make it onto the front page of the *Reading Eagle.*

Readers picked up their papers on December 3, 1893 and discovered that a resident of Longswamp Township sought and secured the services of a Reading "pow-wow doctor" to rid his home of a rug-ripping, bed-tossing, Bible-taunting spirit.

There it was on Page One, upper left corner. Prime time, in newspaper terms.

The unidentified homeowner was vexed by the hex for several months, and was at wit's end until the powwower entered the picture.

The energy within the house had tousled and torn carpets on the floor, produced mysterious footsteps that were heard clearly on the steps, and had caused a bed to shake and squeak when no one was on or even near it.

A friend suggested that the afflicted man place an open Bible on the bed. This, he believed, would intimidate the evil visitor and sent it packing.

Instead, the unseen force seemed to wrap around The Good Book, sending its pages flapping and fluttering before incredulous eyewitnesses.

The frustrated victim turned to the recommendation of another neighbor, and made the trip from Longswamp to Reading.

There, he found the powwower—a gent trained and experienced with supernatural forces, and the ridding thereof.

"When the 'doctor' was asked to explain the

BERKS THE BIZARRE

cause of the midnight invasion," the newspaper article said, "he said that it was a clear case of witchcraft, and that he would soon put a stop to it."

His "cure" was not delineated in the story, but it was noted that the "patient" carried out the orders to the letter.

It is known that the powwower informed his client that the process would take a full ten days.

"Nothing has transpired in Longswamp Township since the (Civil) War that has caused so much gossip as the antics of the spook in the old building," the *Eagle* writer continued. "Many believed the startling stories while others expressed doubts."

The incidents took place just before Thanksgiving 1893, and the writer waxed sentimental as he related the end results.

"The turkey served on Thanksgiving day was one of the juiciest and no feast was ever more enjoyed.

"It was a genuine Thanksgiving day. The family had something to be thankful for and it proved one of the most enjoyable events of the season.

"The clothing in the bedroom is now found in its proper place, the bed intact, and the sparrows seem to chirp and sing about the premises in an unusually lively manner.

"The 'hex' has apparently vacated the premises, and the inmates are now able to slumber in peace."

BB

BERKS THE BIZARRE

CYCLONE!

When it comes to potential devastation and death-dealing weather phenomena, there are no more fearsome words than hurricane and tornado.

But, on Wednesday, January 9, 1889, Berks County—and indeed a great swath of Pennsylvania—was visited by what was then termed a cyclone.

There had never been, and likely has never been since, such a single incident of nature's fury in the history of Reading.

There was every indication that the ghastly storm was on its way.

Federal Signal Service officers had been tracing a major disturbance which brewed in the skies of Texas on Monday. Fierce winds and driving rains continued north through Arkansas and turned eastward at Chicago. Devastation was left in the wake of its two day course.

A bridge at Niagara Falls had tumbled into the river. Factories and residences in several cities were scrambled by the wind.

Just after noon Wednesday morning, raging winds and hail bombed the buildings and pelted the pedestrians of Pittsburgh. A seven-story building under construction at Diamond and Wood Streets was wrecked. Its bricks, girders and wet mortar tumbled onto surrounding structures. Scores were trapped in the rubble. Boats on the rivers were swept away in the 50 miles an hour winds.

The barometric pressure at Pittsburgh plunged to the lowest point ever recorded.

With a vengeance, the storm barreled eastward. Altoona, Carlisle, Harrisburg, Lebanon—each city and others suffered incalculable damage.

The York market house was wrecked. Factories and hotels in Williamsport were reduced to rubble. In the capital, the winds were estimated at 75 miles per hour, and only estimated because they annihilated the anemometer cups on the state Weather Observatory.

BERKS THE BIZARRE

But, it was Reading which would suffer most.

As telegrams were received in Reading, officials did what they could to brace for the worst and warn an unsuspecting public.

The afternoon grew increasingly ominous. From the west, the storm bounded across the foothills and into the Schuylkill Valley.

At about 5:15 p.m., the worse fears of those who had been charting the path of the storm were realized.

The storm roared across the river and took its first toll at the Pennsylvania and Reading Company paint shops near Oley Street. Several men painting passenger rail cars scrambled for cover watched helplessly as their workplace was wrecked and their comrades were burned to death.

A newspaper article detailed the holocaust: "Their companions were enveloped in the embrace of the flames. Their cries were heard for a moment by the terrified workmen, and then their voices were hushed forever. They were quickly roasted to death, and the fire from the nine passenger cars lit up the heavens for miles around."

The tanks of those cars in the shop at the time had recently been filled with benzine. The force of the winds caused each to explode with a deafening fury. Residents throughout Reading scurried to their porches as the blasts rocked the streets. Many feared an earthquake had struck. Rockets of red flames shooting into the clouds of dusk told them something even more unthinkable had happened.

Eyewitnesses said the cyclone swirled savagely in a path about 100 yards wide and made its way toward North 9th Street.

BERKS THE BIZARRE

Roofs spun into the darkening sky. Bricks, shutters, and anything in the twister's way were swept into its spin of death.

The newly-constructed St. Joseph Catholic church on N. 8th Street lost its roof, and neighbors feared the entire sanctuary would be blown to bits.

Then, as a hawk bears down on its vulnerable prey, the cyclone blasted into the walls and windows of the Reading Silk Mill at 12th and Marion Streets.

No place in the city would have been a worse place for such a storm to hit.

A full shift of workers, more than 200 in number, were at their machines. Paint, gasoline and naptha were stashed in unprotected storehouses.

The cyclone dashed its destruction through low residential neighborhoods and slammed broadside into the Silk Mill with an inestimable force.

The 14-inch thick brick walls shattered. Windows were blown to sandy shards. Timbers and beams were cast about like toothpicks.

In the space of perhaps two minutes, the main part of the building became a crater of death and horror. Only the engine room, tower and tall smokestack of the structure were left standing.

As those few who survived the initial wrath of the storm peered through the dust and destruction, they were jolted by an explosion which could be heard and felt in most parts of the city.

What was left of the mill was almost instantly engulfed in a fuel-fed fire.

The winter sky was blood red as rain pounded the scene of terror. Fire alarms sounded throughout Reading and volunteer emergency crews sped to the mill after their assignment at the paint shop. The steady rain helped them drench the flames quickly.

The first to arrive recoiled at the sight. Bodies were strewn between looms and spools. Faint and pathetic cries and moans could be discerned beyond the sound of raging rain and the smoldering blaze.

It was, according to a contemporary report, "a chorus of woe and agony that never before was heard in this city by anyone."

Shrieks of emotion–the wailing of joy and despair–accompanied the throngs of neighbors who rushed to the wreckage.

By 7 p.m., some 5,000 people ringed what was left of the mill. Bonfires illuminated the grim scene as fire fighters trimmed the ruins to prevent any further collapsing of walls.

As they labored, others plunged into the piles to seek out the dead, the dying, and any who had miraculously survived.

Every doctor, every ambulance, and every fire or police service employee was summoned.

One by one, the bloody bodies of the victims were extricated. Corpses of workers, many just in their teens, were placed on the perimeter of the mill.

The desolation was delicate. Any untoward moves on the part of those who entered to rescue survivors or remove victims might cause even more havoc.

By midnight, the bodies of three males and 11 females were taken away and identified. Another 80 individuals were presumed dead in the deep ruins of what had been a sturdy, three-story building.

But, it was still dark–dismally dark. What morning

would bring could never have been estimated by anyone.

Dawn broke on a on a devastated city. It was discovered that rowhomes around the mill had sustained severe damage. Most of those in the 1100 block of Marion Street and the 1400 block of North 11th were ravaged.

The 900 block of Windsor Street sustained major damage, and shade trees were ripped from their roots along 8th and 9th streets.

The Mount Penn Stove Works at 3rd and Greenwich Streets and the J.H. Sternbergh & Son nut and bolt plant were nearly ruined. Luckily, the thick of the storm cut through a mostly industrial section of the city.

Railroad cars were scattered across the tracks of the yard in the center of town and the incinerated bodies of five men were removed from the railroad paint shop.

Crowds continued to build around the ruined silk mill. The Reading Artillerists were summoned by Mayor James Kenney to help keep order, as fire and police leaders organized battalions of relief workers.

"Occasionally the crowd was ordered to keep quiet, and then the rescuers would listen, and the moans of the injured could be heard sometimes close to the surface and then deep down in the debris," a reporter noted.

Tales of horror and heroism emerged throughout the morning.

Little Sadie Shade, critically injured and pinned under a heavy girder, watched in pain as her friend Annie Daver was pulled safely from her less precarious position.

"Good bye, Annie," moaned Sadie. She managed a slight smile as her friend found salvation.

They were Sadie's last words.

The mangled body of a 13-year old girl was found in a thick pile of timbers of the silk mill. Clasped in a death grip in her right hand were her scissors.

Rescue worker John Dengler had already helped remove a half-dozen individuals from the ruins and was turning away to take a break from his labors. At once, he heard a faint moan.

He scanned the wreckage and pinpointed the sad plea. He lifted two giant beams and found his own daughter beneath them.

"Papa!," she squealed in a dying gasp. Dengler gingerly lifted his beloved and held her in his arms–in which she died.

As the morning hours waned, the sun continued to aid the clean-up effort.

The brilliant day also brought out more gawkers and ghouls. An estimated 15,000 spectators looked on at mid-day.

The mill, built recently by the city and leased to the Grimshaw Brothers of Paterson, N.J., was at peak production. In it was an estimated $14,000 in premium silk. As emergency crews had worked in the dead of night, so did thieves who worked their way into the ruins and carried away most of the precious fabric.

Gradually, black crepe ribbons were draped to porches of houses in which the dead once lived.

In the court house, city and county officials pledged funds and material support for the rescue and recovery.

BERKS THE BIZARRE

The Ringgold Band instantly announced it would stage a benefit concert at the Grand Opera House. The manager of the opera house volunteered the site. Throughout the city, clubs, churches and merchants set up relief funds. School children were asked to contribute, and did.

Major General David McM. Gregg, a Civil War hero, took charge of the relief effort. Within a week, nearly $9,400 was collected.

Of course, there was profit to be made from the tragedy.

The New York Photographic Gallery sold a packet of photographs of the eerie ruins of the mill, and a broadside epic poem was composed and sold by an enterprising writer.

If there was any good news in the aftermath of the tragedy, it was that the initial estimate of fatalities was bloated.

By Friday, January 11, every worker in the mill was accounted for. Seventeen died in the mill, five in the paint shop, and more than 100 were injured in the two locations.

A grief-stricken Mayor Kenney appealed for all in the city to rally around their losses.

"The fearful cyclone that struck this city has brought sorrow and want to many of our people, who are in such circumstances as to be unable to meet the emergency, and the occasion calls loudly for immediate action," his proclamation read.

"Quick to respond to others in distress, let us not fail to do speedy justice to our own grief-stricken people."

The building was rebuilt shortly after the disaster,

BERKS THE BIZARRE

and continued to serve as a mill for many decades.

After several years of neglect, the old silk mill was placed on the National Register of Historic Places and converted to a 40-unit apartment complex in 1986.

BB

BERKS THE BIZARRE
EXECUTED...WITH DECORUM

The front page of the Reading Eagle on Friday, the 13th of May, 1870, was almost totally consumed by the long and lurid account of the execution of convicted murderer John Deail.

"On account of the quiet and peaceable character of the population of our city and county," the story began, "an execution for murder is a very rare event...consequently, the present occasion created considerable excitement."

The murderer was Luzerne County native Zachary E. Snyder, a rogue whose background included convictions on horse thievery, rape, and army desertion. In the course of his crimes, he used the aliases of Voltaire Snyder and John P. Deail.

Under the latter *nom de plume*, derived from his mother's maiden name, the 25-year old was convicted of killing vagrant Schuylkill Countian Richard Harlan.

Deail had been released from Eastern State Penitentiary in Philadelphia on October 6, 1869, after serving time on the rape conviction.

The day after his release, Deail was seen in Exeter Township, loitering suspiciously on a farm near the Black Bear Hotel.

Somewhere near there, he met the man he would soon hack to death.

Deail and Richard Harlan passed through Reading and headed north. They imbibed at Graeff's Tavern in Leesport, and in that same village Deail purchased a hatchet in Miller's store.

On October 9, Deail plunged the business end of that hatchet into Harlan's back and neck. His mangled body was found near the Schuylkill River just north of Leesport.

After committing the deed, Deail continued north and was arrested in Orwigsburg after attempting to assault Mrs. Sarah Walborn.

After arraignment before Orwigsburg Justice of the Peace Samuel Madden, Deail was taken to jail in Pottsville. There, he admitted killing Harlan, but claimed self-defense.

A three-day "full, fair, patient and impartial" trial in late October ended with Deail's conviction and condemnation.

In prison, Deail was well-behaved and was visited often by several pastors. Rev. Father Borneman of St. Paul's Roman Catholic Church, assisted in Deail's ultimate conversion to Catholicism.

On April 11, 1870, after Deail was informed that his execution warrant had been signed, he told his jailers that he was prepared to die, because God was his friend.

A month passed, during which Deail was "furnished with all the delicacies he craved."

Small groups gathered around the prison in hopes of spying the doomed man, who, according to prison guards, remained calm and resigned to his fate.

The night before he was to die, Deail asked to have his fingernails trimmed, requested the clothing he had worn the day the murder was committed, and packed his personal effects in a trunk to be sent to his brother in Ariel, Pa. He then retired for a restless night in his cot.

The number of ghoulish gawkers grew around the prison yard early the next morning as Charles

BERKS THE BIZARRE

Henninger brought the black-stained pine coffin through the gates. Police ringed the prison and adjacent fairgrounds to maintain order.

At mid-morning, Father Borneman strode into the prison, followed later by contingents of doctors and lawyers.

Just after noon, Deail ate his last meal and listened as the final touches were put on the gallows. The 16-feet high structure was built in Philadelphia, and Deail would be the 14th man to die upon it.

The first steps toward that death were taken at 1:25 p.m., when John Deail ascended the gallows stairs.

He knelt in prayer with the ministers for about ten minutes, and then turned to the 200 spectators in the prison yard.

"My brothers and friends," he said in a low voice, "I acknowledge the deed for which I stand here, and I am most heartily sorry for it, but I thank my Maker above for this, and I am in full hopes of being encircled in the arms of my Savior."

The somber prisoner then shook hands with the priests and the sheriff. A rope of Italian hemp was affixed over his head, followed by a black hood.

At 1:35 p.m., the executioner pulled the trap. As the *Eagle* article noted, John Deail was "launched into eternity" as he became the seventh person to be executed in Berks County.

"After the drop," the writer noted, "there were a few twitches of the body and limbs. The pulsations of the heart ceased altogether after 12 minutes." Deail's neck was not broken, and it was determined that he had suffocated.

What followed was a bit bizarre.

BERKS THE BIZARRE

After Deail's corpse was placed in the coffin, it was hustled into an outbuilding of the prison yard, where Drs. M. Albert Rhoads and Stanley Smith waited with a bank of wires and a galvanic battery.

An incision was made in Deail's neck, and a wire was inserted into a nerve.

An electrical charge surged into the body. The chest heaved and "sometimes the face made hideous contortions and grimaces," according to one witness.

The experiments were conducted merely to "demonstrate the force of a galvanic battery," and not to revive the dead man.

Despite this strange experiment, the *Eagle* journalist assured readers, "The execution throughout was well conducted, and everything passed off quietly and with proper decorum" on that Friday the 13th of May.

BB

BERKS THE BIZARRE
"A DREAD,
UNEARTHLY VISTITANT"

Deep in the "morgue" of the *Reading Eagle* is the late 19th century report from "a reliable correspondent" about a "dread, unearthly visitant" which was stirring up the citizenry around Kirbyville just after the turn of the century.

At what was described as "the old school house which stands on the Boston Road, between Kirbyville and the Half-Way House", some rather spooky things were going on.

"Even our most trusted citizens here have occasionally seen strange objects and heard strange sounds," said the correspondent.

There were reports of firmly-nailed boards at a nearby home flying off, and a particularly-intriguing episode which involved what the writer described as two "tramps" who sought a night's lodging in the abandoned schoolhouse. We shall join the story at that point.

"When they were in the room some time," it was reported, "one of the men saw that his pipe moved away and off the desk, and could not see what caused it to move.

"Soon, something pulled at their feet, and they were terror-stricken to see something so unusual and terrible as to freeze their very life blood.

"They rushed out of the room into the woods nearby, and slept there the remainder of the night.

"They could not describe the thing they saw, but said it was ghastly and presented an appearance so

BERKS THE BIZARRE

horrible that they were glad to get out of its reach."

The correspondent even provided "reliable sources" of the strange tale.

"This story," the article affirmed, "was related to Stanley J. Kirby, Reuben Hafer and others, and it can be relied on."

The story concluded with a tantalizing teaser: "It is said that a man was once murdered (at the old school house) and his body thrown into its well."

BB

DON'T SWEAT IT!

The night of August 16, 1900 was uncomfortably warm, even on the summit of Mount Penn, where many folks had gathered for a dance in the Tower Hotel.

As bandleader John Fahrbach prepared to lead his orchestra in the night's program, he stunned the crowd.

To the shock of all, he announced that all young men on the dance floor would be allowed to dance without their suitcoats, but only if they were not wearing suspenders.

"Instantly," a Reading Eagle *reporter noted, "a number of coats were dispensed with, while a number refused to dance at all. The latter had come without coats, but neglected to remove their suspenders, and had no belts. It was too hot for them to dance with their coats on."*

Just a week before, the newspaper article said, several young men were ordered off the dance floor because they were dancing without their coats.

On that hot night of August 16, however, maestro Fahrbach made an announcement that was indicative of not only a change in the temperature, but perhaps a change in society itself!

199

BERKS THE BIZARRE
TOMBSTONE TALES

Graveyards are daunting places. And in Berks County, many of them are *haunting* places.

The thought of walking alone at night through a cemetery and becoming disoriented within a forest of tombstones and tangled tree branches—moonlight casting an eerie silvery glow and the calls of nighthawks piercing the silence—has fired the fears of mortals since the beginning of recorded history.

But what about those who tend those cities of the dead?

In 1891, a *Reading Eagle* reporter spoke spooks with John Hepler, the superintendent of the Charles Evans Cemetery—the largest and in its own way, most beautiful graveyard in Reading.

In an article headlined "Among Graves at Midnight," the writer set the tone of the piece with the opening statement: "It is quite safe to say that there is no such thing as a 'spook'.

In the ensuing interview with Helper, who was superintendent at Evans from 1880 to 1907, all notions of graveyard ghosts and ghouls were discounted.

"I have not heard or seen anything to indicate the presence of so-called ghosts or spooks," said the "clear-headed" Mr. Hepler.

"I often read the accounts of those unearthly creatures in the newspapers and often wonder how people can be so superstitious as to believe in them.

"I have passed through the cemetery at all hours of the night and never saw anything like spooks prowling about."

BERKS THE BIZARRE

Hepler, who resided on the cemetery property, affirmed that his family felt quite secure there, and never gave ghosts a second thought.

The superintendent even offered to escort readers through the graveyard any night to allay their fears.

"I would not advise a nervous person to try it," he said, "because the stillness of the place and the new sounds they would encounter would naturally frighten such a person."

Hepler also waxed philosophical about the future. "I hope," he said, "the time will soon come when people will not be so superstitious as to imagine that everything new they see or hear when they pass a cemetery will be called a spook.

"Reading people are not as superstitious as those of some other places, but still some are afraid and hold in terror the thought of taking a trip through a cemetery in the dead of night."

James C. Hart, who has been superintendent of the Charles Evans Cemetery since 1991 and was serving in that capacity at the time of this writing, read with fascination the Hepler assessment.

While he stopped short of sharing his predecessor's zeal for the debunking of things ghostly, he says that in his many years at the graveyard where more than 68,200 souls are at eternal rest, nothing of the supernatural sort has ever taken place.

Hart does admit, though, that when the sun goes down and night falls over the well-guarded graveyard, things out there are indeed a bit daunting.

As for *haunting*, well, that remains to be seen, so to speak.

If nothing else, graveyards have often tended to

attract the eccentric.

Take an incident in 1900 when eyewitnesses at the Epler's Church cemetery watched as a mysterious man made a strange visit to the tombstones during a driving snowstorm.

It was odd enough to warrant an article in the *Eagle* and an accompanying artist's sketch.

The man was about 70 years old, and never once spoke to the many people who passed by and tried to strike up a conversation.

"Some persons are of the opinion that he is partically demented," the account said.

"He was first noticed some days ago when he entered the cemetery and began to read the inscriptions on the tombstones.

"He did this for several hours, then left, but returned."

No one knew who the man was, and some folks believed he was an inmate who had escaped from an institution.

Others thought he may have been a former resident of the area who returned to visit the grave of a loved one.

"Where he spends his nights and obtains his

BERKS THE BIZARRE

meals," the article continued, "is not known.   The old man carried a tablet with him and as he pauses in front of a tombstone he writes down the inscription."

BB

BERKS THE BIZARRE
THE DANCING GHOSTS

She drove past the church cemetery near Five Points every evening on the way home from work in the city.

Never was there any reason for concern as she turned the corner onto a narrow road that led past an undeveloped meadow in a corner of the graveyard.

Then, one night in the fall of 1982, everything changed.

We shall protect the woman's standing on the job and in the community with anonymity, but will draw exact quotes from a recent interview in the cemetery where her unusual experience took place.

As you read this, you will learn how this stroll among the tombstones brought a revelation which rattled the woman and may have revealed the very source of her supernatural encounter.

First, we turn back the calendar a dozen years.

"I was driving home one night and I didn't think anything of it at the time, but I saw three kids playing. I thought, 'What are three kids doing out in the pajamas, in a cemetery, at a quarter to ten at night?' But, I didn't think much more about it.

"A couple months later, I saw the same three kids. They were running around playing ring-around-the-rosie or something, and chasing each other."

At that point, that night, she slowed and took a cautious, closer look. "Something just didn't look right," she remembered.

On a third occasion, she actually pulled over as she once again spied the children frolicking in the dusky shadows.

204

BERKS THE BIZARRE

"They were there, but they *weren't* there, if you know what I mean.

"They weren't glowing, or emitting light, as such, but they were a dullish glow–something like the color of a milk bottle."

Struggling for descriptive words, and constantly regaining her composure, the witness to the weirdness shuffled those calendar pages ahead to the summer of 1994.

"It was a Tuesday night," she recalled, "and my sister and I were driving past the cemetery."

She inadvertently let something slip: "Did you ever see those ghost kids in there?"

Her sister's eyes bulged. With that, she knew that her sister had also seen the spectral siblings cavorting in the corner of the cemetery.

They decided to contact this writer and reveal the story.

There's not much more to that story than what has just been detailed.

The women found it hard to estimate the ages and genders of the visions.

As the three children are all dressed in what can best be described as "long pajamas," the woman could not ascertain their sexes.

"I would estimate that they're all between five and ten years old," she said. "I see them very briefly, and they kind of run off into the woods. I would have figured they'd run into the cemetery itself, but they don't."

She shook her head and admitted that she was at once embarrased to tell her story and baffled as to what it all means.

BERKS THE BIZARRE

We headed back to our cars, weaving through the tombstones as we walked and talked.

As I glanced at the grave markers, I was taken aback by something that seemed to leap from the cold granite into the depths of my imagination.

With little emotion, I asked: "Have you ever tried to find a possible source of the ghostly kids?" My eyes were cast downward to a trio of tiny tombstones.

"Not really," she replied as she turned her own attention to what had drawn mine.

"Oh, my God," she recoiled as she examined the inscriptions on the polished stones.

Three abreast were the graves and the names of brothers who each died on the same day, at the ages of five, six and ten years.

The woman claimed she had never seen those tombstones, or those names, before.

She nervously asked, "Could this be them? Could these be the children I have seen?"

"Maybe now," she continued, "I know their names."

As we reached our vehicles after lingering at the three graves, our conversation tapered into small talk.

There really wasn't much more to say.

At least not there, and not then.

BB

BERKS THE BIZARRE
CHILLS AT CHARLIE'S

All conditions are condusive for a haunting at Charlie's, the charming restaurant along Route 422 between Baumstown and Douglassville.

It was once the Ben Franklin Inn, and it's along what is officially the Ben Franklin Highway.

Ben never dined there, slept there, or came anywhere close to the place. But, the property has been inhabited since the good doctor's day.

Tracing the deeds of the land, names like Penn, Jones, Boone and Ludwig can be found. Examining keystones and carvings on the building, dates like 1808 and 1824 are evident.

Charlie's restaurant has a past. And, if its chef, its barkeeper, and its proprietors are to be believed, Charlie's also has a ghost or two.

It would be difficult to discount their claims, given the preponderance of things that thump in the night and disappear by day.

The present proprietors of Charlie's are John and Paula Bauer. It was at their invitation that this writer dropped by to hear about the many unexplained incidents and unexpected surprises within the walls of the ancient building.

The most ancient walls envelop a comfortable downstairs dining room. That original section of the enlarged former residence dates to 1749.

The first known addition was made in 1809, and the most substantial enlargement was made in the 1970s, when the building was converted into a restaurant and took on its current dimensions.

After nearly two decades as the Ben Franklin Inn,

the Bauers took over and named the restaurant after John's father, Charles.

With unabashed pride, Paula Bauer showed us through the five dining rooms of the establishment. Bedecked with antiques and collectibles, and lavishly decorated chambers with names like the "Country Room", the "Candlelight Room", and the "Tavern Room" are appointed in styles which range from Edwardian and Laura Ashley to Budweiser and Coor's Light.

Paula pointed out that the building is situated on a plot of land which also includes a large farm to the south and a small schoolhouse to the east. A side road now bisects what was once a tract granted to its original owners by William Penn.

Legends abound on the property. It is said that an old Indian burial ground lies somewhere on a line between the schoolhouse and the restaurant.

And, there is evidence that what is now Charlie's was once a stop on the Underground Railroad. Southern slaves seeking freedom were once given refuge there.

The Bauers, their chef, and other employees believe the supernatural sensations there may be centered in a room just over the Charlie's barroom.

Oddly enough, it wasn't until the Bauers had occupied the building for several months that the room was discovered.

In a building which also boasts a concealed staircase and other architectural peculiarities, there is a secret room in which it is speculated that the runaway slaves were accommodated.

"We'd been in this closet a thousand times and

never thought anything of it, and never knew or noticed what was behind it," Mrs. Bauer said as she peeled back clothing and other items to reveal the low doorway to the hidden room.   There are at least two schools of thought when it comes to the notion of a ghost at Charlie's.

Michael Bachman is a believer.

Mike left his native Shillington to explore a career as a chef in far-flung places. He settled back in Berks County and took the job at Charlie's. His skills in the kitchen are among the very best anywhere, and his brushes with the unknown at Charlie's are among the most baffling.

"After a busy Saturday night, we were winding down. Just the waitstaff and a couple people were at the bar. One of our waiters and I were sitting at a table in the corner of the main dining room, just relaxing.

"The lights were out in the dining room. All of a sudden we heard running upstairs–diagonally from one corner to another. Well, you can't run diagonally because of the layout of the rooms and walls up there.

"We looked at each other. We thought it was a little strange. I said maybe it was our dishwashers horsing around.

"But, a few seconds later, they came bursting through the double doors. They didn't see us, because the lights were off.

"I asked them if they had been upstairs, running around. They said no. Then, we heard it again. Running, back and forth. So, we all went upstairs, two of us on one flight of stairs, two on another.

"Nothing."

That inexplicable incident was but one of many.

BERKS THE BIZARRE

"It was the middle of an afternoon," Mike recalled. "We were just sitting around. One of the waitstaff jumped out of her stool. She said that something had brushed against the back of her neck. Sure enough, the hairs on the back of her neck were standing out.

"And as she stood there, the jukebox turned on. Nobody was anywhere near it."

There are only two ways to start the jukebox. No one was close to either switch.

As those in the room gasped, they looked at the digital readout on the jukebox. Usually, only two figures are displayed. That time, the number "1937" glistened on the panel.

"The next thing we knew," Mike continued, "hats started flying from pegs just above the jukebox. At that, the waitress flew out of here like a shot!"

"People see things upstairs in the corners of their eyes," Mike said. "They have seen somebody walk past an open door. They call out, thinking it's another employee. But, there's never anybody there.

"We've had our shirts tugged on every once in a while, and when we'd turn around, there'd be nobody there."

Mike remembered another incident which had several employees puzzled.

"It was about ten in the morning, and I was the only one here," he said. "I went back in the kitchen to grab a bucket. I headed toward the sink and it was like I put my hand through a wall. I jumped back. My whole hand and the bucket started to vibrate. It was a very strong force, whatever it was.

"I didn't say anything to the guy who came in

210

about ten minutes later. So, he came in and I told him I wanted to show him something.

"He took the bucket and went to the sink. He went, 'Wow! What the hell is that?' I told him I didn't know. For about two minutes, he and the bucket, well, vibrated!

"If you would put your hand down or touch something, it would stop, like it was grounding or something. One day we had the whole waitstaff back there experiencing it."

That bizarre occurrence continued for two or three days. "I don't know if it was just a coincidence," Mike said, "but it was all during the phase of the full moon.

Ruthanne Seiders is Charlie's amiable bartender. Having previously toiled at the former Brinton Lodge, another Berks restaurant with a history of hauntings, one would think "Ruthie" would be a true believer.

Well, even though she had two or three experiences with the unseen inhabitants at old Caleb Brinton's place, Ruthie remains the eternal skeptic.

"I gotta say that I don't believe in these things," she said...nervously.

And, while she would like to discount ghosts, poltergeists and supernatural energy, she is a storehouse of strange tales.

"I was closing up one night," she remembered, "and heard faint music coming from the vestibule. I walked over, and the music got louder.

"Then, it softened and got louder again."

Ruthie was certain that the music was coming from within the building and not from a passing car or nearby residence.

BERKS THE BIZARRE

In fact, it seemed to come from the second floor of Charlie's. Then again, when she started upstairs, it faded. The source of the sound still has her perplexed.

So, too, does an episode which took place in late summer, 1994.

Several employees heard the distinct and loud sound of glass shattering in the kitchen. They immediately went into the kitchen to investigate, and found nothing disturbed. There was no trash being collected, no recyclables being sorted. Nothing.

Ruthanne Seiders says she and patrons have heard footsteps on the floor just over the bar—the floor of the empty and barely accessible "slave quarters". She has seen shadowy figures where there is no one, and has heard the footsteps and music on several occasions.

And, while she disavows any belief in unseen entities, she often finds herself talking to them—chastising and chasing them.

"Maybe I don't want to believe because I'm often here by myself," she said.

Our visit to Charlie's proved inconclusive. No footsteps were heard, no shadows, no tugging and no music. Still, we left with a viable story of the unexplained.

Not long after that visit, the telephone rang.

It was Ruthanne Seiders, down at Charlie's.

She wanted me to know that just after I left the restaurant, two patrons said they heard footsteps on the floor over their heads.

As those around the bar pondered that sound, all jumped as the speed rack—a bottle rack firmly attached to a sink—crashed to the floor.

BERKS THE BIZARRE

For that to happen, the rack would have to lift itself up and pull itself out. That's exactly what it–or an unseen force–did.

"Never in all my years of bartending did a speed rack come off like that," Ruthie said. She later pointed out how it is virtually impossible for the rack to become dislodged as it did, on its own.

Whatever may or may not haunt Charlie's has not tormented any of those who have enjoyed a fine meal in one of the pleasant dining rooms.

Then again, maybe someone has heard phantom footsteps or has seen an elusive shadow, and never knew others have, as well.

Now they know, and perhaps will tell their tales.

BB

BERKS THE BIZARRE

ABOUT THE AUTHOR

Charles J. Adams III has written books on ghost stories and legends in the Pennsylvania Dutch Country and Pocono Mountain regions of Pennsylvania, as well as in Cape May and Long Beach Island, N.J., and the Delaware shore.

He has collaborated with David J. Seibold to write and publish other books about shipwrecks along the New Jersey and Delaware coasts and train wrecks in eastern Pennsylvania.

His latest effort was a collaboration with Beth E. Trapani, *Ghost Stories of Pittsburgh and Allegheny County.*

A morning radio personality on WEEU in his native Reading, Pa., Adams is also a travel writer for the Reading Eagle newspaper, and is very active in the Reading and Berks County community.

Adams serves as a trustee of the Reading Public Library and a member of the council of the Historical Society of Berks County.